Best Practice:

Everything You Need to Know About Starting Your Successful Private Therapy Practice

By Kate Aronoff, MA, LPC

Printed in the United States of America

First Printing, 2017

ISBN 9781520463223

Aronoff Counseling
2300 14th Avenue SE
Albany, OR 97322

www.AronoffCounseling.com

To Greg and Mom. You give me the courage to try and the resilience to get back up again when I fail. Thank you for your unrelenting support.

Table of Contents

Welcome!

Do you love the feeling you get after an amazing therapy session with a client? That high that comes from knowing you've just really helped someone move along their life's journey in a healthier and happier way? It feels so good to know you are making a deep and meaningful difference in people's lives....Then comes the harsh reality of a micromanaging boss, a tiny paycheck, nasty office politics, and an unmanageable caseload to completely kill your sweet therapeutic buzz.

Imagine being able to achieve those intense moments of helping and bonding with your clients – and never again having a job you didn't love. Never again having a boss to report to. Never again gazing at job posting boards and wondering if there might be an agency out there that could treat you better. Never again feeling like you're merely a replaceable cog in someone else's machine.

You can have that! And it's not as fantastical as it might sound. We are fortunate in our profession as therapists that we have the ability to strike out on our own and form our own private practices. You can build the job in which you get to do the work you love to do, set your own hours, and manage your own caseload.

If picturing all of this makes you want to do a happy dance, that's great! You've got that entrepreneurial spirit, which will help inspire you along this journey of starting your very own business. If picturing this also terrifies you, I take that as a healthy sign. You're human, and making a big life change is scary. A healthy dose of fear can help guide you on this path of business ownership to avoid making careless decisions. But don't let that fear hold you back from moving forward to accomplish your dreams.

I am here to walk with you through the fear of starting your practice. I will break down the process of starting your business into manageable steps. With this guide, you will be able to build your business quickly and with minimal frustration.

Ticket to Ride

Starting a private practice as a therapist can often feel like riding one of those old wooden roller coasters – the ones where you're certain the 90-year-old screws holding it together might come loose at any moment.

There are extreme highs where you find yourself jumping for joy in the bathroom at your current workplace with the thought of getting out of there and being your own boss; those times when the world feels like your oyster, just waiting for you to dive into the ocean and pluck out the pearl that changes your world.

There are also the low points, when you question your ability to help yourself, let alone other people. Who would trust me to help them with their problems? How could I think I would be able to run a successful business?

Then, there are the opinions of others, to which you become extremely susceptible. One little comment can make you question your career choice completely, or cement your conviction that you were destined to become a counselor and entrepreneur. For example, someone once told me that I was a "real-life hero." That brought a tear to my eye. Hell, it brought ten tears to my eyes. Emotions run rampant up and down the hills and valleys of the roller coaster ride of starting a private practice.

Remember, when you are in those dark times of doubt, that you are a "real-life hero." Stick with it. You can do this! And I am here to help.

Stumbling Upon Success

In starting my private practice many years ago, I felt like I was embarking on a road trip with no map. I knew where I wanted to end up, but wasn't sure of the route... Or even how to get out of the driveway. I was constantly trying to piece together little tidbits of information from the internet and the people I knew in the industry about how to start and run my business.

next. A mentor of mine gave me the idea of starting a private practice during my internship, and something about it felt right. I knew I no longer wanted to work full-time for someone else. I was tempted by the notion of creating something great from scratch. But I knew I also needed time for my practice to grow and provide me a steady paycheck - not to mention experience to feel confident treating clients on my own.

I decided to start my practice one day per week, and work at an agency the other 4 days of the week for a few years. This way, I got the stability of a regular job while getting to work on my goal of expanding my practice.

As I worked to build my practice over the years into the full-time job it is now, I would often get together with my colleagues in private practice. We would share information to try to help each other through the "maze" of running a business. While my colleagues were incredibly helpful, I often thought, "There has to be a better way. Why isn't there a simple guide that I could just follow to navigate all of the ins and outs of owning my practice?" I wanted that road map.

About This Book

Well, consider this your very own road map! I have put together this handbook to save you countless hours, headaches, and perspiration trying to piece together this information on your own, like I did. Because I am a champion Type-A list maker, I have broken steps down into manageable to-do lists for you.

I know many of you are probably working either full- or part-time at your day job while you get your side hustle on with your private practice, so it's crucially important to save any time and effort you possibly can. I've also included many templates of forms you will need in this handbook, so you don't have to create everything from scratch – a time-consuming process, I assure you!

A quick note and then we can be on our way to creating your successful practice. The advice and suggestions in this handbook are based on my experiences, discussions with colleagues, and guidance I have received from mentors along the way. It is the product of a collective of knowledge that I have gathered in my own brain over the years. I am eternally grateful for the wisdom of those colleagues and mentors who have shared their insight with me along the way. I certainly could not have gotten to where I am today on my own.

Along these lines, I want to make it clear that I have not received any "kickbacks" or monetary incentive from anyone or any company that I reference or recommend.

I sincerely hope this handbook will make the process of starting your practice easier and actually fun so that you can let your creativity, personality, and expertise shine!

Chapter 1

How Do I Actually Start a Business?

First things first: A great big kudos to you on becoming an entrepreneur and venturing into what might be new territory for you. Taking the initial steps toward owning your own business is very exciting indeed. To properly set up your new business, there are several legal and logistical aspects to consider that may not exactly inspire you. Though, I promise there will be passion-inspiring tasks later on! This chapter addresses each of the regulatory hoops you must jump through to be able to open up your own practice. Time to get your jumping shoes on!

Choose a Name for Your Business

Well, let's first start with a fun task to get the ball rolling. Choosing a business name is one of the more exciting aspects of starting a business. You get to use your imagination, and fulfill any dreams you may have had as a budding entrepreneur during childhood.

Cue the brainstorming session! No filters. No judgment. Let the ideas flow.

After you've narrowed it down to some winning names, there are few logistical concerns you'll want to consider before you officially title your business:

1. Is your desired name already taken? You'll want to check the name you want hasn't already been snagged. You can do this by searching for your chosen name on the following free tools:
    a. A general web search using a search engine like Google.com.
    b. The US Patent and Trademark Office's search tool at https://www.uspto.gov/.
    c. Search for the domain name (a.k.a. web address or URL) that you want to use on a site that sells domains, such as GoDaddy.com or Wix.com.
    d. Your state's business filing office (SBA.gov, 2015)

2. Does your name portray the brand image you want it to? Run your name by some friends and family members to see what their reactions are to it.

3. Will you use your own name in your business name? You do have the choice to use your own personal name, or to file under another name, known as "doing business as" or DBA for short. A wise mentor once encouraged me to use my own name as part of my business name, so that clients and colleagues who know me will be able to find my business information online easily. I have found that when I go to refer a client to one of my colleagues, I have an easier time remembering and locating their website when it has their personal name in it.

   If you have a difficult name to spell or an unfortunate name, like Robert Butts, I advise you to go the creative route; although, "Butts Counseling" would certainly be a memorable name. I apologize to any Butts who are reading this now. However, I'm sure this is not your first rodeo when it comes to growing a thick skin for name jokes.

   Besides having an unfortunate name, there are other arguments for choosing a non-personalized name for your business. For example, you may decide to change your last name after getting married or divorced. You may also want to sell your business at some point in the distant future. It may be easier to sell "Inspire Counseling" rather than "Aronoff Counseling" to a young budding counselor. I know this seems far, far down the road, but it could actually happen at some point. You could ride off into the sunset, retired, with a check in hand. Daydream about that for a minute….

4. Some states, such as California, may have certain rules about the business name you choose. This is rare, but they may require you to use specific words, such as "counseling" in your business name. Check with your state's business filing office to make sure you meet any requirements before you finalize a name.

LLC, S-Corp, Sole Proprietorship. What are they? Why do I need to know about them? I just want to provide therapy!

Before you begin to "therapize," you've got to register your business with the powers that be. I often hear from folks in this field that they feel very anxious about the process of registering their business. I assure you: you're smart. You got through graduate school. You can do this.

Now, you will first have to figure out which type of business incorporation option is right for you, the choices being:

- Sole Proprietorship – This is the most basic of the options. You, alone, are responsible for the company and all assets and liabilities.

- Limited Liability Company (LLC) -- Protects your individual liability in the company, and offers some tax benefits. This is probably the most common type of business incorporation for private practitioners. An LLC may not be an option in all states, such as California.

- S-Corporation (S-Corp) – You are taxed only on a personal level. This can be a good option if you have employees, or even if you don't. There may be tax benefits in this category if you earn an income above a certain amount. An S-Corp is probably the second most common choice for private practitioners.

- C-Corporation (C-Corp) – Generally more complex, and recommended for larger companies.

- Partnership -- You might use this option if you are starting your practice with another person. There are different types of partnerships to choose from.
  (SBA.gov, 2015)

Choosing a business incorporation type is an area where I recommend consulting an accountant. You really can do the vast majority of business establishment tasks yourself. However, every business situation is different, so I cannot advise you on which incorporation type will be best for you. I've found there are a multitude of varying opinions out there about which type of business registration is best. Thus, it's probably a good idea to get a professional's opinion – one who can examine your particular situation. And you're going to want to establish a relationship with an accountant anyway, so it's not a bad idea to do that at the get go. To find a reliable and trustworthy accountant, I recommend soliciting word-of-mouth recommendations from friends and family.

I can tell you that, for me, an LLC was the way to go at first. An LLC is akin to the middle of the road option. A sole proprietorship is pretty bare bones. You don't have much protection from someone suing you if you go that route. I'm a cautious person, and I just didn't feel like I wanted to take the risk of that happening. An LLC gives you more protection from a client coming after your assets in a malpractice suit. They can only sue you for whatever your company is worth, not what you are worth personally. That said, you'll want to make sure to have liability insurance to cover both yourself and your LLC. This is covered more in-depth in the section on liability insurance.

After starting with an LLC, I later switched to an S-Corporation (S-Corp) status a few years into owning my practice. As my practice became more successful, I was advised that there would be a tax benefit to switch to being an S-Corp. This is because you do not have to pay both corporate and employee income taxes under an S-Corp designation. An S-Corp does not pay federal taxes at the corporate level (BizFilings, 2016).

Be aware that you will have to do an official payroll if you have an S-Corp, even if you are the only employee. You'll need to have an accountant manage payroll unless you know a lot about accounting. You have to set up your withholdings for taxes, Social Security, and Medicare. And you will also have to file quarterly reports to the IRS as part of payroll. It's beyond my level of accounting skills, and likely beyond most therapists' skill set. Based on quotes I have received, payroll management by an accountant costs about $35-$50 per month

Regardless of which business designation option you choose, you can probably complete the registration with your state on your own (rather than hiring an attorney or accountant). You can also get assistance from online services like Legalzoom.com for a fee.

The cost of registering your business can vary greatly from state to state. Registering an LLC can range from $50-$800 (Costhelper.com, 2015). To find out what the fees are in your state, visit your Secretary of State's website.

You may also be required to file for a business license in your county. Some counties require you to register your business, and then pay county taxes. Check your county's website for more information about this step.

Publishing Your Business Formation

In some states you may be required to publish notification of the formation of your business in the newspaper. This usually costs about $40-$100. (Costhelper.com, 2015). You should receive this instruction to publish if it is required when you file your business incorporation with the state (i.e., the previous step).

Operating Agreement

An operating agreement is a little known document that no one usually talks about, but is pretty darn important. In fact, many states require one for LLCs. An operating agreement is a document that outlines the duties of all members of an LLC. The reason for its importance, is that an operating agreement may be used in court to prove you have a legitimate business which is separate from your personal assets. In short, it could save your hiney from being sued, and losing your house, car, and little junior's college fund.

Luckily, it's quite simple to come up with an operating agreement. There are templates online. You can also ask a business law attorney to help create and/or review yours to ensure it would stand up in court. Make sure to keep a copy of your operating agreement on your computer and in a safe place.

A Note About Liability Insurance

If you haven't already done so, you will want to purchase professional liability insurance for yourself as a provider. This protects you from losing boatloads of money when a client decides he is less than satisfied with your services. But did you know that your business entity (LLC, S-

Corp, etc.) may not be covered under that insurance? Call your insurance company and ask that your LLC be added to your insurance plan. The cost will be a little higher, but you will be more comprehensively protected should a disgruntled client decide to rake you over the coals in court.

Getting an Employer Identification Number (EIN)

You will need to apply for an Employer Identification Number (EIN) with the Internal Revenue Service (IRS) for tax purposes. You will use this number to get paid by insurance companies or employee assistance programs (EAPs). You will also use it to file taxes. It's pretty important. It's very easy to get, too. You just need to go to IRS.gov to apply for one. It is free to apply for an EIN.

Chapter 2

How Do I Set Up an Office?

Once you've established your business as a legitimate legal entity, it's time to find a place to set up shop. Even if you choose to do mainly online counseling, you will still likely need a physical location to meet clients for the first time, as many states require face-to-face contact prior to switching to remote communication. Make sure you are aware of your state's requirements on this, if online counseling is your plan.

Office Space

Finding an office can feel incredibly daunting. There are so many factors to consider, like:

- How much can I afford to pay?
- What part of town would be best?
- How many other therapists are in the area?
- How do I find part-time space, if I don't want to see clients full-time?
- Do I feel safe seeing clients here, especially in the evening or on weekends?
- Will there be a receptionist to greet clients?
- What is the waiting area like? Will my clients feel comfortable waiting here?
- How private is the space? Will I be overhearing loud arguments from the divorce attorney's office next door? (Some of this may be mitigated by using multiple white noise machines, but not always. A tip: try using a white noise machine both inside and outside your office door for best results.)
- Will I get to arrange and decorate the space as I want to?

Before you develop a full-blown panic attack about this, practice some mindful breathing and positive visualizations. You may not find the *perfect* space, but I am willing to bet you will be able to find something that works for you. Here are some guidelines for choosing an office:

- **Location, location, location**

  You may notice that many therapist directory sites, like PsychologyToday.com pull search results based on zip codes. Keep that in mind when choosing an office location.

  If possible, try to choose an office in a desirable zip code. What do I mean by desirable? I mean a specific area with a population with whom you would like to work. Picture your ideal client. Now where do you think they might live? For example, if you want to work with children, choose an office location in a zip code with a high population of young families. If you enjoy counseling people who deal with chronic illness, choose an office near a large medical complex.

  If nothing came to mind, don't worry. You can actually contact your local library for help with this….for FREE! Who knew? Libraries have access to databases that can help you determine the demographics and general purchasing habits of people living in different areas. At first, when reviewing the data, it feels a little creepy that "Big Brother" knows I enjoy purchasing pet products for my dog, but such is the techie world we live in. Why not embrace it and put it to use?

  Another trait of a desirable location is having fewer therapists per capita than surrounding areas. Rural areas or newer suburban developments are often underserved by mental health professionals. Thus, they make good areas to set up shop. To determine which areas are less saturated with therapists, you can do a Google Maps search for "therapist *(your potential location)*" to see how many dots show up on the map. You may want to avoid an area where the dots are clustered together.

  Another strategy that has worked for me is having two part-time office locations in two different zip codes. This means that when potential clients search for a therapist online, usually using their zip code, your profile would pop up in the search results for twice as many clients. That equates to double the amount of referrals for you. That's what I'm talkin' about!

- **How Much is This Going to Cost Me?**

Office space rates can vary greatly. A lot depends on the location. It may benefit you to choose a pricey office if it is in a more affluent area where you could charge higher session rates. On the other hand, having low overhead by saving on an inexpensive office could really help your bottom line. You have to find the best option for your practice.

When you are first starting out in private practice, it can be immensely beneficial to get part-time or pay-by-the-hour space. No, I'm not talking about a seedy by-the-hour motel room – get your mind out of the gutter! I mean co-working spaces, wellness centers, or group practices that may allow you to pay an hourly rate for space. This way, you won't pay any rent above what you need. So, if it takes longer than you anticipated to build your caseload, you're not losing money. Of course, with this option, you may have little control over the arrangement and décor of the space you're using. Hourly rates also tend to be a more expensive option once you hit a certain number of hours per week. So, keep an eye on your costs as your business grows.

The other cost-saving option I mentioned is renting part-time space. This is usually done by subletting with at least one other person. For example, you may only need space on Mondays, Wednesdays, and Fridays, and could share with someone who wants space on Tuesdays, Thursdays, and Saturdays. In this case, you could be the original renter or the sub-letter. Good office mates may include other therapists (especially if they have a complimentary specialty to yours), psychiatrists, mediators, family law attorneys, or holistic practitioners. Think outside the box when searching for an office mate.

But Do I Really Need to Shell Out For an Office?

Some budget-conscious therapists have gotten the notion that having an office in their home or meeting clients for walks in the park is a good alternative to paying rent for a brick and mortar space. Doing this can bring up a whole host of issues! For example, while the vast majority of clients are highly unlikely to pose any safety risk to you, there is a small chance of something bad happening if a client knows where you live. Perhaps, a client could show up at your house for some impromptu therapy around 2 am? Or worse. If you're still thinking a home office is a good idea, please go watch the movie *What About Bob?* for reference as to how a client can intrude on your home life.

Meeting clients in a public place, like a coffee shop or park, sets the stage for a breach of confidentiality. Anyone there would be privy to know that your client is seeing a therapist. They might also eavesdrop on your conversation with your client to learn the juicy details of their inner life. There may be some exceptions when meeting clients in public would be warranted with the client's informed consent to do so, but they are few and far between. It is definitely not an effective means for saving on overhead costs.

How to find an office

The internet is your friend in this arena. Here are some ideas for searching for space:

- Check out Craigslist.com.
- PsychologyToday.com has a section for therapists to post available office space.
- Networking events with other professionals could be a good way to find out about office space opportunities.
- Put the word out to friends on social media sites like Facebook and Twitter that you are seeking office space.
- Search online for wellness centers, co-working spaces, and group counseling practices in your area. Then, contact these places to see if they have space for rent.

Receiving mail

Getting a P.O. Box has been recommended to me by other therapists, but I haven't done it. My reasoning for this is that I don't think I would check a P.O. Box frequently enough. Instead, I get mail sent to my office address. This way, I get mail throughout the week. The downside of this became clear to me when I moved to a new office. Although I made every attempt to forward my mail, many items got lost. This created a logistical nightmare when trying to get insurance companies to reissue lost checks to me. I am still cleaning up the mess nearly one year later. So,

I can now see the benefit of having a P.O. Box, which would not have changed with my across-town move. If you think you would check you P.O. Box regularly, you may want to go ahead and get one. The United States Postal Service website (https://www.usps.com) has more information about how to get your own P.O. Box, along with prices based on size.

Phone service

Until you reach a level where you are able to hire an assistant, the easiest thing to do is to use your personal cell phone for business phone service. Many in our field will tell you that you must have separate business and personal phone numbers. It's good boundaries.

I was in full agreement, until just recently when I started to question this notion. Now that our smart phones have the capability to be set to "do not disturb" settings that will only allow callers you want to get through, I'm not entirely convinced that separate phone numbers are necessary anymore. This "do not disturb" technology prevents work/life boundary issues, like middle of the night client calls waking you up while you're getting your much needed R & R. You can also block numbers if you have a caller who won't respect your boundaries. A downside is that with only one number, you may end up screening your calls more often. I never answer a call from an unknown phone number unless I'm prepared to talk to a potential client.

HIPAA compliance should be on your radar when setting up a phone account. Regular cell or landline phone service is considered less "hackable," so it is the preferred method of communicating with clients. The creators of HIPAA rules do not appear to appreciate the internet or anything new in the realm of technology. It seems they would like us all to be communicating with two tin cans and a piece of string.

Setting up a secondary line with your cell phone provider is one option that appeases the HIPAA gods. When I contacted my cell phone provider about this, they quoted me at $25 per month for a second line. They told me I could use an old phone that I had lying around to be connected to this new line. You must have a second phone to use if you go with this option, as two lines cannot go to the same phone or device. Twenty-five dollars per month adds up fast, so I went in search of a cheaper alternative.

When I discovered I could get a free Google Voice account with a separate phone number for my business that gets forwarded to my personal cell phone, I thought it was a no-brainer. (To set up an account, go to google.com/voice.) I've recently come to learn that Google Voice is not technically considered HIPAA-compliant, since it uses the internet to transmit calls – something called Voice Over Internet Protocol (VoIP). I thought I was still covered, since I had signed a Business Associate Agreement (BAA) with Google. A BAA basically means that Google vows it will protect your information to the level required by HIPAA. I recently discovered that there is a fine print loophole in this BAA, in which Google Voice is carved out and excluded from the BAA. What?! Not cool.

Do not lose hope in the free option altogether, my fellow cheapskates. I see Google's loophole, and I raise them two more potential loopholes! One potential work around to the VoIP issue is to switch your *personal* number to the Google Voice phone number. Have your family and friends use the Google Voice number to get a hold of you. You would then use your cell phone number as your business number. So all client calls would go directly to your cell and avoid VoIP altogether. I can't actually take credit for this genius idea. It came from an article on this very topic, "Therapy Business Line on the Cheap?: HIPAA and VoIP Services" (Huggins, 2016).

A second loophole is to adjust your settings within your Google Voice account to forward all calls straight to your personal cell phone number and turn off call screening. This way, you still have a separate phone number to use for your business line. I emailed Google's help desk to find out if this option would indeed meet HIPAA standards, and was met with an "I don't know" answer. I have scoured forums on the subject, and still come up empty-handed. This method appears to completely bypass the VoIP route, as no calls or voicemails register on the Google Voice account page. This loophole may not be as HIPAA bulletproof as the previous loophole mentioned, as I cannot get full confirmation from the Google pros that it does not use VoIP during a call or voicemail. However, I feel that it's worth considering.

I sometimes hear about other free phone applications that some therapists use, like Sideline or Grasshopper. These programs also use VoIP, and are, unfortunately, not HIPAA compliant. At this point in time, the best options are to pay for an extra cell phone line, use a conventional landline, or use one of the Google Voice loopholes described.

Communicating via text messages with clients must also be viewed through the HIPAA lens. And guess what? The HIPAA gods don't like it. What a shock! The method of sending text messages does not comply with HIPAA standard safeguards. You need to avoid texting any Protected Health Information (PHI). You could potentially text clients if you are not communicating any PHI. But that could be difficult to enforce. For this reason, I find it easiest to just avoid texting altogether with clients, and stick to phone calls and voicemail. I have never had anyone balk at this. If you do decide to try texting with clients, make sure you get their permission to do so first in writing.

A quick note about client phone calls: A pet peeve of mine is hearing from people that they have gotten up the guts to call therapists to begin treatment, only to get no response at all. Not returning calls is totally unprofessional. It gives the public the message that therapists don't care, and it is a major hurdle for folks to get help. Many just give up after not hearing back from several therapists.

It may be hard to fathom a future where you would ignore a phone call from a potential new client. But one day, your schedule will be full, and you will be short on time for returning phone calls. It sounds so amazing, right? Don't get too cocky when this happens. You still need to present a professional and positive image to the public. Do yourself and others a favor by adding a statement to your outgoing voicemail message saying that you are not accepting new clients right now, or that you have a wait list. It's an efficient way to let people know you're full without having to make time-consuming phone calls. I also recommend adding your local area's crisis phone number to your outgoing voicemail message to ensure clients know where to go for support when you are not available.

Computer

You'll want to have a reliable laptop for your practice. A small, lightweight one is nice to have, since you may end up carting it around quite a bit. You could conceivably use only a desktop computer, if it works for you logistically. However, I find I need to be mobile with my files.

In order to be HIPAA-compliant, you'll want to have a password on your computer. This should be a no-brainer these days, but you know what they say about assuming. You should also password protect any documents with client information.

You will definitely want to back up your computer files to an external hard drive to prevent a major emotional meltdown if your computer crashes. Hard drives vary in cost based on the amount of storage space. You likely won't need a large quantity of space, because yours will be mainly smaller files, like short documents. I write more about this in a later chapter, but I keep most of my notes in an electronic medical record online called Simple Practice (www.simplepractice.com). However, I still have many forms and other documents that I would not want to lose on my computer.

It is also advisable to encrypt and password protect your external hard drive. You can do this for free. Here is a website with step-by-step instructions for both Windows and OSX - https://answers.syr.edu/display/software/Encrypting+your+external+hard+drive+on+Windows +and+OSX

Email:

Email can be a quick, easy way to communicate with clients about a host of topics, like rescheduling a session, sending an invoice, or doing a brief check-in to ensure their mental wellbeing between sessions.

Again, you'll want to be sure you are using encryption with any email that contains protected health information (PHI). I started using Google Apps for Business (https://gsuite.**google**.com) to encrypt my messages. It costs $5.00/month. Google Apps also gives me an email account with my business name in it (i.e., kate@aronoffcounseling.com rather than kate@gmail.com). This helps your email appear more professional. It is relatively simple to set up, with the phone support provided by the fine folks at Google. The downside is that incoming emails are not encrypted. I always let my clients know this in my disclosure form, and get their permission to communicate via email beforehand.

You can also get a stand-alone encrypted email platform that will encrypt both incoming and outgoing emails, such as Hushmail. These platforms usually have a higher cost, but are certainly a secure option.

Faxes

Unfortunately, the therapy field has not realized it's the 21st century yet. Most of us are still using fax machines as a primary mode of communication. A likely reason for this is we are all too scared of violating HIPAA laws with technology, and too busy to figure out another safe way to communicate about clients. The bottom line? You'll need to be able to at least *send* faxes.

I have recently moved to an office where I cannot receive faxes, and nothing earth shattering has happened yet. You may be able to get away with not being able to *receive* faxes in this day and age with minimal upset to the flow of business.

You might have faxing capability as part of your office space agreement. Some landlords may charge a small fee to use the fax machine. Others may include it in your rent. You can also set up a fax machine at home. I found this was costly to do, as you usually need a landline. Who has those anymore?

My solution? I send faxes using a free service called Doximity.com, which is a website for healthcare professionals. I scan in documents to my computer, and then fax them online using Doximity.com. Unfortunately, there is no way to receive faxes on Doximity.com.

Office Supplies

Luckily, there aren't a whole lot of supplies you will need to set up your practice. Many of them, you may be able to pilfer from around your house. You will likely need the following:

- **Printer** - It is nice to have one with scanning features, especially one that has a feeder tray to scan in multiple pages at once. I have found that black and white is fine when it comes to printing, but you may want to spring for the color option if you like colorful documents. You may also want to get one with faxing capability, because you will be sending and receiving a fair amount of faxes. However, if it can scan documents, then you can at least *send* faxes through a Doximity.com (see Faxes above).
- **Ink cartridges or toner**
- **Printer paper**
- **Lined paper** - I use this to take notes during assessments, but it's certainly not a required office supply.
- **Stapler and staples**
- **Paper clips**
- **Pens** - Shell out for some quality ones that you like. I've found there can be great joy from having a good pen. If you've ever worked in an office, you know there are the reject pens that no one wants, lurking in the main office supply drawer. They're just waiting to stop working in the hand of the next unsuspecting new employee. You are your own boss now, and dammit, you deserve the fresh, colorful, gliding pens to do your important work.
- **Address labels**- Believe it or not, I still snail mail quite a few letters in this day and age. You can order a ridiculous quantity of them for a very low price from VistaPrint.com. You may want to order them at the same time as your business cards (discussed in Chapter 5: How Do I Sell My Services?).
- **Postage stamps**
- **Clipboards** - I would suggest getting two or three. This way, you can have one for each member of a couple or family. You can also leave the extra one out in the reception area for your next client.
- **Notepads** – I use these for writing to-do lists and making a list of upcoming clients and session plans each day.
- **Paper Shredder** – to shred anything with protected health information on it.
- **Tissues**

Decorating On the Cheap

One of the more fun parts of setting up your office is decorating it however you want to. Time for an HGTV binge session! But you just started your business, and cash flow has yet to begin, so that floor-to-ceiling zen fountain you've envisioned may have to wait. Here are some tips for decorating without breaking the bank:

- A coat of paint can go a long way towards making an office your own.
- Embrace your inner discount shopper. Visit stores like Home Goods, Ross, IKEA, and Tuesday Morning to find wall art, furniture, rugs, etc. Online shopping at Wayfair.com has been successful for me, especially when they have sales and coupons.
- Craigslist is an excellent source for the more expensive pieces like desks and chairs.
- Make sure to measure your office space before you purchase that big sofa.
- Leather or faux leather is your friend. It tends to be more cleanable than other upholstery fabrics. Trust me, you will want to clean it from time to time. You never know what your clients will come in with. I've encountered bed bugs, bathroom accidents, and even one woman who went into labor while sitting in my chair. Keep some leather wipes and air freshener on hand!
- Decorate with your clientele in mind. Choose décor that is relatively gender neutral. For families or couples, you may want to have a loveseat or couch, rather than chairs. If you see children, you'll want to have some kid-centric art, and toys, of course. The Dollar Tree and consignment stores are both great for finding budget-friendly therapy art supplies, toys, and games.
- Arrange the furniture with safety in mind. Always ensure your seat is closest to the exit, based on the very slim chance that your physical safety becomes threatened and you need to escape. Seat backs should not be facing the exit, as this can make clients with trauma histories feel unsafe.
- Avoid harsh lighting. Fluorescents are the worst! I like to get several lamps with warm yellow bulbs to make it feel more like a home than an interrogation chamber. Just make sure it's not too dim in the space so that clients don't feel unsafe. Dim lighting can be a trauma trigger.
- Windows are great, but we are not all so fortunate to score an office with one. Luckily, you can create the feeling of a window by adding a curtain rod with curtains to a solid

wall. You can even add a picture or faux window frame between the curtains to complete the illusion.

Creating Forms

Being in private practice means you get to create tailored forms and customized processes to suit you and your needs. This is a very good thing. However, it can also be frustrating to make everything from scratch. That is why I have attached my personal forms and templates that you can use. These ready-made forms will save you countless hours and frustration, and can be altered to meet your needs however you wish.

See the appendix for the following forms:

- Intake form
- Disclosure form
- Release of information form
- Treatment plan template
- Fax cover sheet

Disclaimer: I make no claim that these forms will stand up to legal standards, as these vary greatly from state to state, and are often changing. You may wish to run them by an attorney to ensure compliance. I provide these forms as a time-saving tool to get you up and running with your own forms.

Online Counseling

With so many tools available online now, it is no wonder that online counseling is gaining in popularity. Counseling online can be a great way to cut costs on overhead, such as office space. It also allows clients to access therapy from the comfort of their own homes, making transportation, inclement weather, illness, and other barriers obsolete. The convenience of online counseling may also encourage clients to seek counseling who may not have otherwise done so.

There are several media for online counseling – video, chat, and email. Unfortunately, online counseling is not as simple as one would hope when HIPAA gets involved. You'll need to think about making your video, chat, and email HIPAA-compliant. This means "getting your encryption on."

If you who have no idea what I'm talking about (like me a few years ago), encryption basically scrambles your messages while traveling across the Interwebs so that they can't be intercepted as easily by hackers. HIPAA compliance means that a platform uses at least a 128-bit level of encryption to prevent hackers from getting access to the information. You'll want to ensure that you use a platform that asserts they are HIPAA-compliant so that you are doing your due diligence to ensure protection of your clients' information.

For the video and chat options, here are a few platforms that I would recommend. I would not recommend using free video software. Free versions usually do not offer technical support, which is an absolute must. Some video platforms may offer a few sessions per month for free, and that is a good deal. Beware of platforms that are all free, though. Of note, Skype.com and FaceTime do not purport to be HIPAA-compliant.

- SecureVideo.com- This site costs about $25 per month for up to 8 sessions, or $50 per month for unlimited sessions. At the time of publication, they were also offering 2 free sessions per month. They have a Business Associate Agreement (BAA), which is important for HIPAA-compliance. Having this agreement with them ensures your clients' information will be protected and they will not improperly access it or leak it. You can also bill your clients for their sessions through PayPal or Authorize.net on this site. Secure Video also gives you the ability to keep your session notes on their site.

- VIA3.com- This platform does both video and chat. They assert that they are HIPAA compliant. Their technical support folks are available via chat, and will call you if you like, during business hours. Video quality is good, without a delay like you can find on Skype. Cost is $29.99/month

.

- Nefsis.com- The cost is $49/month. They have a free version, but it doesn't have any technical support available.

Many of the video platforms will offer a demo or orientation session first before you have your first session. This is a good way to ensure you know what you're doing with the technology before you try it out with a client. You can and should also test them out on family and friends too, to get familiar with what the process was like for them. This way, you can help walk clients through simple troubleshooting.

Medical Records

There are many online practice management programs out there. I strongly suggest you use one! Using a program to schedule appointments, send automatic reminders, keep client records, and track billing will make your life better -- I promise. I use one called Simple Practice that I find easy to use and reasonably priced. Feel free to ask around to your colleagues for their recommendations, too. Make sure you find one that sends some form of automatic reminders to clients for their sessions.

I also scan in any paper documents into Simple Practice through my printer/scanner. I shred them after I do that, which gets rid of so much extra paper I would have to find storage for. I highly recommend scanning records, or you will quickly end up with a house full of filing cabinets. Plus, this method makes documents easier to search for and find.

You'll also hear many folks in the field talk about using Office Ally. I also use Office Ally to submit insurance claims. You can also use it for keeping medical records and scheduling. The best part about it? It's free! The user interface is a little wonky to use at first, but fairly simple once you get the hang of it. Their customer support has been helpful to me on more than one occasion when I need something out of the ordinary, too.

Out-of-office coverage

One unfortunate thing about private practice is that we don't have a co-worker down the hall who can cover for us when we are away from the office. Here are a couple of ideas for how to handle being out of the office:

- <u>Send an automatic out-of-office email response to anyone who emails you.</u> I have one that goes out to everyone all of the time stating that I will respond to their email within 24 business hours. This message provides crisis numbers for those who need urgent support. I change the message when I am out of town to reflect that, and I provide coverage numbers if applicable (see below).

- <u>Have an out-of-office voicemail.</u> Similar to my email, I have a standard voicemail that tells clients I will respond during business hours, and provides crisis numbers for after-hours support. If I go on vacation, my voicemail message will also include instructions on who to contact in my absence.

- <u>Find a trusted colleague to back you up when you go on vacation or leave.</u> Especially if you are going to be out of the country or in a remote area where you will be disconnected from technology (good for you!), it is important to get another therapist to serve as backup for your clients in your absence.

  <u>Having a trusted backup</u> also enables you to fully relax and not worry about your clients needing support while you are out. Fill that chosen colleague in about any safety concerns or other important issues you anticipate might arise before you leave. Always be mindful of HIPAA and disclosing protected health information when you do this, of course.

- <u>Have a statement in your disclosure form about your general availability.</u> If you are not available on nights and weekends, let clients know that boundary from the start. Provide a crisis number or other instructions about what they can do if they do need support when you are not available. Your personal time is precious - protect it as such.

Consult Your Peers

While setting up your business, you will likely begin to realize that you could really use some input from others who are in the same boat. Being in private practice can be very isolating sometimes. That's why it's incredibly important to have regular contact with other professionals in the field. Joining a consultation or supervision group can provide you with support for tough cases, general ethical guidance, and camaraderie.

To find a group, put out feelers to friends or colleagues you already know in the field, letting them know you are looking for a group to join. If you are new to an area, you may also find a group online on PsychologyToday.com, MeetUp.com, or Facebook.com. If you can't find a group to join, make your own! Others are probably jonesing for connection just like you are, so they will be apt to join a group if one is created.

Chapter 3

How Do I Manage the Money I Make?

Accounting

I have no idea how I survived math classes in school – and got good grades, no less! It seems to me that my mathematical skills have completely vanished in my adulthood. It turns out that knowing how to find the cosine of an acute angle in an isosceles triangle in 10th grade trigonometry does not necessarily translate to bookkeeping skills for a small business. Darn.

If you are like me, and accounting is not your strong suit, you may want to consider some options for keeping your books in your practice. It is important that your financial records stay organized and up to date. So if you are not up for the task on your own, you must find a way make sure it gets taken care of. You want to ensure you're paying appropriate taxes and not spending more than you make. With that said, here are some options to help you in this often tricky realm of accounting:

- <u>Purchase accounting software.</u> Quickbooks is probably the most popular one on the market. With this option, you will still have to do a fair amount of managing your own books. You will have to enter every payment you receive, and every expense you have. The software helps to keep it all organized. Cost for Quickbooks depends on whether you get software online or download it to your computer. Quickbooks Online costs about $10 per month, and the desktop version is about $200 in a one-time fee. Keep in mind when purchasing that you will have to upgrade to a new version of Quickbooks every few years.

- <u>Hire an accountant.</u> The price for this varies quite a bit. I have been quoted around $100-200 on a quarterly basis ($400-800 annually). As I mentioned in Chapter 1, you will likely want to hire an accountant to do your taxes for your business. Managing your books (day-to-day income and expenses) is another level of accounting. This could be done by the same person, or a different person--often at the same accounting firm. If your business is an S-Corp, you have payroll to manage too, which could also be done by this person.

- Hire a part-time administrative assistant. I often run into colleagues who have hired someone part-time to manage their books. This is a cost-effective solution. Sometimes you really only need someone to work 1-3 hours per month on your books. If you pay them hourly, it could be as little as $20 per month. You can likely find folks to do this kind of work via word of mouth from other colleagues. Or, you may wish to use a virtual assistant – someone online in some other part of the world who does freelance assistant work. Some websites to check out for this service are zirtual.com and upwork.com.

You may be able to manage your books on your own when your business starts out, and later transition to a different option as it grows and becomes more complicated.

Financial Considerations

It's a good idea to open a business checking account right from the start. This way, you'll keep all of your business transactions separate from your personal account. The IRS definitely looks favorably upon this. It's a nice way to avoid getting into hot water with them – a good thing to avoid. It should be relatively easy to open a business checking account at your bank. You will likely have to visit the bank in person to open it, and you will need a copy of your EIN Tax ID number when you go. This is a number you get from the IRS when you first register your business (Chapter 1).

Your bank may require additional business documents to open an account, so check with them before you go. You'll also need to deposit a minimum amount of cash into the account to get it started, so be prepared to front some money and pay yourself back later.

Be sure to consider the details of the account before you open it. Ask them what fees may exist for going below a minimum balance or for depositing a large number of checks, for example.

Here's a good list from Nerd Wallet that shows a list of free business checking accounts for each state - https://www.nerdwallet.com/blog/banking/find-free-business-checking-account/

Accepting Credit Cards

It would be nice if everyone paid us in cash, of course, but in this day and age, your business had better be able to accept credit cards. Luckily, it is easier than ever to take plastic. Companies like Square and PayPal have card readers that connect to your smart phone, so that you can take card payments from your office. If you use one of these options, you will get charged a percentage of each sale in fees from the processing company. This is a smart option for those who won't be making very frequent credit card sales, since you only pay for the sales charges you have (rather than a monthly fee). To get a card reader, you would indicate that you want one during the process of opening an account with Square or PayPal.

Another credit card billing option would be to use a company that provides a card reader that connects to your computer, and connects through a website. In this case, you may pay to lease or buy the card reader. This may be a better option if you have a high frequency of transactions (woohoo!), as the fees may be lower for a higher number of transactions.

And a third option for credit card billing is to use a practice management program, such as Simple Practice, which will process cards online and link it to your electronic medical records. A benefit of this option is that you can more easily track billing and appointments in one program, rather than going to a separate website for billing and scheduling.

My advice is to compare rates amongst these options and find the most cost-effective solution for you.

Credit Card Fraud Liability

As of October 1st, 2015, the laws changed as far as who is liable for credit card fraud. It used to be that the credit card processing company was liable if fraud occurred. Now, it is the business owner's responsibility to prevent fraud. That is, unless you have a newer card reader that reads the chip and PIN on credit cards; if you have this type of reader, you are not liable for fraud.

Some companies are charging quite a bit for chip card readers. Square is charging $29 as an upfront fee. PayPal charges $149 for this EMV card reader, and provides a $100 rebate if you charge at least $3000 in the first 3 months of use. While the risk of your business having to deal with fraud is slim, it seems prudent to protect yourself as much as possible with one of these readers.

Taxes

Another harsh reality of having a small business is paying quarterly taxes. That's right. That's FOUR times per year! What the heck, IRS? If you have another part-time gig somewhere other than your practice, it may make sense for you to still only pay taxes once per year. Taxes vary widely depending on whether you are married or single, have dependent children, have another job, etc. You are going to want a knowledgeable accountant to dig into your personal situation and let you know what the best tax payment plan will be for you.

You will need to submit a W-9 form to any company that will be paying you, such as insurance companies and EAPs. On this W-9 form, you will need to include your EIN number, which you have previously received from the IRS. This form basically tells other companies the information they need to be able to officially pay you. So you will want to be sure you have an up-to-date one on file with all companies. You will submit it to them as part of your initial application packet when you first get started with working with insurance companies or EAPs. Many will send you one to complete, but you can also find a blank W-9 form to complete at www.irs.gov. You should update it anytime you change addresses.

At the end of each year, any company that paid you $600 or more will have to send you a Form 1099. A Form 1099 serves as an official record of payment over the course of the year. You will give those Form 1099's to your accountant to file your taxes. In addition, you will have to issue a Form 1099 to anyone YOU paid $600 or more to – such as a landlord for office space rent. You can order the forms and complete them yourself in January of each year at IRS.gov or pay your accountant to do them (I was quoted $55 for this service by my CPA).

You will get to deduct many business-related items off of the amount you owe on your taxes, also known as a tax write-off. Here's a bit I love from one of my favorite TV shows of all time about the mystery of tax write-offs:

Write-offs are one of those things that we hear about, but we're not really sure how they work. Basically, a write-off lowers your amount of taxable income. For example, if you paid yourself $50,000 a year in income and have $10,000 in write-offs, you would only be taxed on $40,000 in income. Having a knowledgeable CPA can be invaluable as they help you navigate these unknown waters. You'll want to keep careful track of spending and save all receipts. See the list of items that may be tax deductible in the Appendix.

Payroll

I have gotten varying advice from CPAs on payroll. As you may recall, payroll is something you have to do officially if you have an S-Corp. Some CPAs have said that issuing payroll for your business is something you only have to worry about once you're making pretty decent money in your practice – like around $60,000/year or more. I've had another CPA tell me that is false, and that you must do payroll regardless of income if you have an S-Corp.

Whether or not you do an official payroll, you can still technically pay yourself. Thank goodness, because we've all gotta eat, right? Your withdrawals from the business checking account would be considered distributions rather than a salary or payroll. You also don't need to worry about doing payroll if your business is an LLC or Sole Proprietorship. You would just take your payment as distributions.

If you get to the point where you think you may need to do payroll, which is essentially the act of officially paying yourself and/or partners a salary, you'll want to consult with a CPA to discuss details of it and get it all set up.

Retirement Savings

You can and should set up a retirement savings account for yourself if you are not otherwise doing so in another part-time job setting. This is important. Just because you're not working for a big company doesn't mean you shouldn't be saving for your future. Self-employed folks can set up a few types of tax-deferred savings accounts, including:

- A Simplified Employee Pension (SEP) retirement savings account, in which you can save up to 25% of your net earnings
- A One participant-401K account
- A Savings Incentive Match Plan for Employees (SIMPLE IRA)

You will need to contact your bank or other financial institution to get one of these accounts set up. There are specific forms you will need to complete, depending on which plan you choose (IRS, 2015). You may want to talk to a financial advisor to decide which type of savings plan is right for you and your specific situation.

Disability Insurance

I would recommend purchasing disability insurance if you are not otherwise insured by another employer. Disability insurance will cover up to 60% of your income if you can no longer work for health reasons. Be aware that most insurance plans will exclude maternity leave, so don't count on it to cover you if you birth and begin raising a new human being. Don't ask me how they decided that wasn't a valid enough medical reason!

There are many companies that offer disability insurance. When evaluating a plan, make sure to choose one that will cover you if you can no longer work as a therapist (called an Own Occupation plan). Some plans will only cover you if you can no longer work in *any* occupation. You should also shoot for a plan that covers you until the age of 65. Ideally, it should also be guaranteed renewable, meaning the company can't change the terms on you in the future. If you can't find a plan with all of these standards, it's still better to settle on a plan that's less than perfect and have some insurance rather than none (Frankle, 2014).

Health insurance

Since many of us still get our health insurance coverage through an employer, you will want to think about this important benefit for yourself. You may be fortunate enough to have a partner or spouse whose employer-subsidized health insurance will cover you. Get on board that train if you can!

If not, you will be largely on your own to find and purchase health insurance for yourself and any children. Unfortunately, the options out there are not all that affordable for self-employed folks. You may have noticed (if you have seen any news source in the past decade), that the political climate around healthcare coverage is ever so slightly volatile. Ha! In fact, most of us have no idea what to expect about what health insurance will be like in the coming years. A website that may be useful as a guide is the U.S. Department of Health and Human Services FAQ's page (https://www.hhs.gov/answers). There, you can determine whether you might be eligible for Medicaid healthcare coverage (government subsidized health insurance for low-income families), as well as find other information and updates on healthcare reform.

Chapter 4

How Do I Start to Work with Insurance Companies?

Insurance Panels

Ah, the age-old dilemma of whether to accept clients' insurance or not. Many a therapist's Facebook group has debated this issue, filling the comments section with a range of emojis. There are so many opinions about accepting health insurance in private practice. I strongly suggest you solicit any and all opinions about the subject, and then form your own.

What you will likely hear is that the main positive aspect of accepting insurance is the steady flow of clients you receive. That is pretty much the only reason why anyone agrees to work with insurance companies. Since having a full caseload is paramount to us making a living, many therapists have agreed to work with insurance companies despite the drawbacks. The most commonly discussed downsides are:

- More paperwork
- Time spent on the phone or online sorting out benefits eligibility and claims
- Lower payment rates than for self-pay clients
- Restrictions on length and number of sessions

The good news is that you can change your mind about whether to accept insurance, because you are your own boss. Also, you can dip your toe in the water with one insurance company and see how you like it. You don't have to commit to all insurance all of the time!

Let's explore more about what it looks like to contract with an insurance company. Being a participating provider on an insurance panel means that you have signed a contract with them. By signing the contract, you agree to accept a lower negotiated rate of payment for their members. This rate varies greatly by company and location. Why would you agree to lower your rates like this? Well, it can be tough to find clients who are willing to self-pay and forgo using their insurance. As I mentioned previously, contracting with an insurance company, it can be easier to fill your schedule with clients.

As much as I sometimes hate working with insurance companies, I know my practice would struggle without them. When I first started out, I was unable to contract with insurance companies since most would not accept me, as I was not a licensed professional counselor yet. I was working on getting my supervised hours towards licensure. During this time, I was able to join one EAP panel, which helped my practice grow somewhat. As soon as I got my license (and contracted with insurance companies), my practice really took off.

I hope to one day be free of insurance companies and only accept private pay clients. However, for most therapists who are starting out, insurance companies are a necessary evil to make a living. I certainly know colleagues who have been successful without ever making any deals with the devil (oops, I mean insurance companies), but it is an uphill battle. The usual route most therapists take is to at least start out contracting with some insurance companies, and try to switch over to private pay as their practice becomes more established.

If you do decide to take insurance, it can be tricky to get them to accept you on to their panels. Not only are you agreeing to lower your rates to that which the insurance company deems appropriate, but you also have to beg and plead for them to let you do that! Doesn't seem fair, does it? It's not. Such is the world we live in. You *can* negotiate with them on rates, though. You can ask for higher rates when you are initially offered a contract, as well as after you've been a participating provider for a length of time.

Requirements

As I mentioned, most insurance companies require panel members to be licensed. Some insurance companies also require a certain number of years of experience to be added to their panel. However, I have heard of pre-licensed clinicians being able to bill insurance if they are supervised by a licensed clinician on their panel. By all means, try it.

Another hurdle to getting paneled with insurance is that many companies are at full capacity for providers in urban areas. This means they are not adding any new clinicians to their panel. You can try reapplying every 90 days to see if there is an opening. I have had some success in appealing this rejection by touting my specialty areas and pointing out a need for more therapists in a certain geographic area. Don't be afraid to push for what you want!

There is one possible way of getting around this no-room-at-the-inn issue. If you get paneled through your work for another agency, you may be able to add your private practice under your name as an additional location. This would be an alternative to being paneled as a completely new therapist. Not all insurance companies will allow this, but some will. Let me add that I am not condoning this tricky move (do you hear that, authorities?), but I've heard rumors of it being done successfully in far off lands.

Getting Started

Figuring out which insurance companies to try to join and who to contact can be tricky, indeed. There can often be different insurance companies that are popular in different areas. How can you figure out which companies are popular? There are several ways. Basically, you start snooping.

- Try to get in touch with a successful therapist in practice in your area and ask them which companies their clients are covered by.
- In smaller areas, you can also find out which companies employ large numbers of the folks in that city or town. Then, go to their company websites to find out what health insurance coverage they offer their employees.
- Look at other therapists' profiles on PsychologyToday.com who work in your zip code, and make a note of which insurance companies they list as being in-network for.

Be aware that smaller insurance companies are often owned by a larger company. So, if you contracted with the parent company, you would be considered in-network with the smaller one too. Your best bet may be to apply to join some of the main large insurance companies, which include:

- Optum/United Behavioral Health (Optum.com)
- Anthem Blue Cross/Blue Shield (Anthem.com)
- Cigna (Cigna.com)

- Aetna (Aetna.com)

Applying for insurance panels can be incredibly time-consuming. Each company has a lengthy application that you must fax in, along with a pile of supporting documents. You will also need to:

- **Create a CAQH profile online.** Go to CAQH.org to get started with this database, in which you document your education, contact information, qualifications, etc. Don't ask me what the CAQH acronym stands for, as I can't seem to find it. We sure do love our acronyms, don't we? Insurance companies can then access CAQH to verify this information and ensure they have your up-to-date information. Go to CAQH.org to apply.

  I am still unclear about why a CAQH profile is required, as I have yet to encounter an insurance company who actually uses it and doesn't require their own lengthy forms. But they say it must be done, so we all must jump through that hoop.

- **Apply for a National Provider Identification number (NPI).** Go to https://nppes.cms.hhs.gov to apply. You may also need to get a group NPI number for your practice, especially if you have multiple employees. From my understanding, most billing and contracting can be done with only an individual NPI.

I found the entire application process to be terribly cumbersome. So, I hired someone to do it for me. Yep, that's a thing you can do. I paid several hundred dollars for a woman who is much more patient than I am to submit and follow up on the various applications. It was worth every penny to save the time and exasperation of keeping track of all that paperwork. The company that I used is currently slammed and I have heard they are difficult to pin down now. An alternative company to try is Alchemy Credentialing at alchemycredentialing.com.

Always Be Confirming

A word of caution: Make sure you are actually paneled with an insurance company before you tell a client you can take their insurance. All of the bureaucratic red tape required in the process can mean that you get word you have been accepted (cue the bittersweet jumping for joy), but they somehow lose any record of you in their system. This can create an embarrassing moment when you have to go back and tell a potential new client that you were wrong, and cannot actually accept their insurance. This is not a fun experience, and it has happened to me on more than one occasion. A simple takeaway – Always call to confirm.

Along the same lines of confirming your participation on a panel, you will also want to confirm each client's coverage, copay, and deductible prior to your first session. You can do this online with some insurance companies. But for many, you still have to do the old-fashioned wait-on-hold-while-listening-to-smooth-jazz thing. When they do finally answer your call, you will need:

- Client's name
- Client's date of birth
- Client's insurance identification number
- Client's address to verify eligibility

So make sure you gather these pieces of information during your initial contact with the client.

Some savvy (and perhaps moneyed) therapists will hire an administrative assistant to verify insurance for them, so that they do not have to wait on hold with that jazz music. This certainly could prevent a lot of time lost.

I've also heard some therapists say they don't verify insurance ahead of time, and inform clients that they will be responsible for covering any costs the insurance company denies. I dread the challenge of attempting to collect from clients after the fact, as many have an uncanny way of disappearing when an outstanding bill is floating around. Go with what you think might work best, and then try another option if that doesn't work.

Please take note that a billable diagnosis from the DSM is required to be submitted to insurance companies if you expect to receive any payment from them. Most diagnoses in the DSM are billable. Where you may run into trouble is when you use Z codes to try to bill insurance. Z codes, such as "Problems in relationship with spouse or partner," are used to describe issues of concern related to a mental health disorder. Insurance doesn't consider them to be enough of an issue to pay for treatment. If you use a Z code as a primary diagnosis, that claim will undoubtedly get denied.

It is important that clients understand this from the start. Clients may not wish to use their insurance (and do self-pay instead) if they know that a certain mental health diagnosis would be on file in their medical record. Couples should also be aware that you cannot bill their insurance if their issue doesn't involve some sort of DSM disorder. So, a couple who merely fights frequently and doesn't have any other issues going on, would not be able to use their insurance to pay for sessions.

I try to make this clear to my clients. I always review their diagnosis with them, usually during our first or second meeting. I believe clients should know what they're being diagnosed with, so that they can be educated treatment consumers. They should be aware of what health information is being given to their insurance company, too. I have had some clients request to switch to self-pay during these discussions, which is great that they are able to make an informed decision about their care.

Employee Assistance Program (EAP) Panels

EAPs support employers and employees in maintaining a healthy and productive working environment. The employer pays for EAP services, which often includes a limited number of free sessions (typically 3-6 sessions) with a counselor for the employees and their family members. The intent of EAP services is to provide either short-term problem resolution or assessment and referral to another type of service.

Joining an EAP panel can be a good way to get clients in your door, especially when first starting your practice. It is usually a bit easier to join an EAP panel than an insurance panel. The paperwork and billing are also usually much less cumbersome. And some EAPs will accept pre-licensed clinicians on their panels.

The process of contracting with an EAP is very similar to contracting with an insurance company, but often there is less paperwork and time involved. To find popular EAPs in your area, follow the same recommendations in the "Getting Started" section of this chapter regarding insurance companies.

As much as I respect the EAP community and their mission, there are some down sides to being an EAP provider. The pay rate for sessions is often lower than that for insurance, and certainly for private pay. Also, the length of treatment is brief, by definition. Thus, you end up doing a large number of time-consuming assessments, only for your clients to wrap up a few sessions later. Some clinicians may also dislike this type of short-term counseling, and may feel they are not able to get into deep therapeutic issues. I find EAP work to be dynamic and rewarding most of the time. I suggest you try it yourself to find out if you like it or not.

There is a trend towards EAP clients being self-referred for longer-term therapy to the same clinician they began with after they have exhausted their EAP sessions. This is a departure from the traditional EAP model, which would have involved referring out to another provider for longer-term therapy. Different EAPs have varying responses to this newer practice – some encourage it and some vehemently oppose it. It is smart to ask an EAP what their policy is about this type of self-referral when you first get paneled with them, so that you don't ruffle any feathers.

Many health insurance companies have an EAP portion of their services. Often, employer companies will purchase EAP services as a sort of add on to their health insurance plans. So, when you are applying to insurance panels, you may also want to apply to their EAP panels at the same time. There is usually a separate application, though. On the plus side, your form completion skills will be on point!

If you decide to become an EAP provider, you may want to get some training on the subject. Training is not required, but I recommend it since EAP work is different from typical therapy. This is particularly important if you plan to provide critical incident services (for responding to serious events in the workplace) or management consultation (consulting with managers at companies about employee issues).

The International Employee Assistance Professionals Association (EAPA.org) is a great resource for all things EAP. They have online training available for therapists interested in becoming EAP providers.

A Note about Treatment Plans

Having started out in the EAP realm, treatment plans were not something that I had to do for my clients. I hesitate to admit this, but when I first got started, it was not entirely clear to me that I must complete a treatment plan for every client in my private practice. I later overheard some watercooler gossip about another therapist who hadn't done consistent treatment plans either. The discussion was about how ridiculous that person was for not having done them. I quickly returned to my office, red-faced, and made sure all of my clients' plans were done in a flurry of activity!

In this profession where we often do not have clear guidelines to tell us what to do, let me save you some trouble: you should create treatment plans for all of your clients. It is considered standard practice to do so, and you'll be very glad you did if you ever get audited by an insurance company. You won't have to submit them to insurance companies, but they would want to see them in the charts if they do come knocking on your door. I recommend doing treatment plans for self-pay clients, as well. Also, it's a very good idea to review and update your treatment plans with your long-term clients every 6 months. A basic template for treatment plans is included in the appendix for your reference.

Chapter 5

How Do I Sell My Services?

Marketing Materials

When I first started my practice, I thought it was vital that I have an array of fancy marketing materials to present to colleagues and clients. However, like many of my initial thoughts about private practice, this has gone out the window.

I advise folks to go minimalist on spending for marketing materials, at least at first. You don't need shiny brochures, magnets on the side of your minivan, or mugs with your face on them – as tempting as those are to purchase! Who doesn't want their own face staring back at them as they sip their morning latte?

Business Cards

Business cards are really the only necessity, in my opinion. And, luckily, you can get a boatload of business cards very cheaply. Vistaprint.com has consistently been the least expensive company that I have found to order business cards and all things marketing from. Bonus: they often offer discounts for new customers. You can also try searching for VistaPrint on RetailMeNot.com and see if there are other discount codes that you could use.

Logo

You may want to develop a logo to help create a brand for your practice. This is certainly a worthy venture, but doesn't need to happen right away. I'm sure many marketing gurus will spiritedly disagree with me on this, but I don't feel my logo has been vital to my practice's success.

When you do feel ready to develop a logo, you can have one designed for you by an expert fairly inexpensively. You can ask your colleagues for recommendations for a graphic designer. Or, you can go online to a site that has designers who will create logos for your business based on what you say you want. You then get to pick the one you like best from a bunch of different designers. One website that does this is 99Designs.com and costs around $300. Another option is Fiverr.com, where creative services start at just $5. Each designer charges a different rate, but you should be able to walk away with a new logo for under $45.

Creating a Website

Unless you happen to be a web designer-turned-therapist, creating a website can seem like a very daunting task. If you don't already know how to read and write HTML code, and the thought of trying to learn it makes you queasier than the teacups ride at Disneyland, you're not alone. The bad news is that having a website is imperative in today's marketplace. The good news is that it is not as difficult to get one up and running as you are probably thinking.

But why do I really need a website?

The answer is simple: because you want clients, and clients shop online for therapists. I cannot believe the number of therapists in practice who do not have a website these days! How do they get any business?

I was chatting with a friend recently who said she had been searching for a therapist for the first time in her life. She said her EAP gave her a list of therapists' names and numbers to try. My friend said she felt overwhelmed and fearful about having to choose a name on a list to share her most vulnerable inner thoughts and feelings with. She said, "How can I choose one without so much as seeing a picture of them or reading a blurb about them?" Because of this, she ended up going to the ONE therapist on the list who had a website. She felt significantly more at ease having been able to read about and see her therapist's friendly face before committing to a full session with her. You want to be that therapist who stands out from the list of faceless names with a stellar website!

Ok, fine. How do I get one?

There are countless options for website creation these days, ranging from low-tech to very high-tech. But before you do anything, you'll need to choose and purchase your domain name. This is your www.bestcounselorever.com web address where people will go to find you online. It's like your street address in the web world. You can't choose one that anyone else already owns. (Incidentally, bestcounselorever.com is available.) Most likely, you'll want it to be the name of your business.

There are a million and one companies that sell domain names. You may want to purchase it from the same company you choose to host and/or design your site. They often offer package deals. Domain names are cheap to buy (hooray!), and you usually have to pay annually to keep the name.

Once you have a domain name, you are ready to start designing your website. Here are a few of those low- and high-tech options to consider:

1. **The easy-peasy on-a-budget route:** If you're like me, HTML code is about as understandable as Greek, Latin, and Mandarin all mixed up together. What is HTML code, you ask? Yeah, you want to go with this easy option. HTML code is the language in which websites are written.

   After several hair-raising attempts at building and managing a website, I discovered this easy-peasy route, which I strongly suggest you follow if you're in the not-so-tech-savvy club. With this option, you create your own website using a simple template. These templates are made so that, if you are relatively familiar with cutting, pasting, adding text boxes, and adding images, you can create a respectable-looking website with little consternation.

   The downside of this option is that you have less control over the features on your website compared to other options described below. You also will pay more than if you go with Wordpress.com, which is free (see option #3).

   With this option, you would pay an agency to host your site, as well. Hosting means your site will be active and available for people to access online. There are likely hundreds of agencies offering this service now, and it's tough to pick one.

I use Wix.com, which I have found to be very easy to use, and they offer protection from hackers ruining your site. GoDaddy.com is another example of this type of website creation, however, I have found it less user-friendly. SquareSpace.com is yet another site of this type, but I have gotten feedback that it is slightly more challenging to use than Wix.com. The cost for this type of website is about $60-$200 annually.

2. **The easy-peasy expensive route:** Pay someone to build, host, and manage your website for you. You can do this with an independent contractor or go through an agency. The excellent thing about this is you don't have to do much of anything. You can sit back, eat Cheetos in your sweat pants, and tell someone what you want them to do! And often, the person or company designing the site will manage your website to ensure it's in working order.

   This, of course, comes at a price. Parr (2015) estimates the cost of a first website designed by a web agency for a small business is $5,640-$11,400. I don't know about you, but that seems like a lot of cash to front for a business that has no clients yet! I am certain you can find agencies and individuals who will do it for less, but the quality and process may be less than desirable. An agency to check out for reasonable pricing on web design is Winterwebmethod.com.

3. **The semi-technical route:** Create your website yourself using a site like Wordpress.com. You can still use templates (either free or purchased) for this option. The templates often have more flexibility than in Option #1. However, you will need to know or learn something about HTML code to effectively manage a site like this. You can purchase website templates from various vendors online. A template provides a framework for how your website will look, and you fill in the content specific to your business.

   Another downside of using Wordpress.com, in particular, is that these sites are vulnerable to hackers. Who would care to hack my little private practice site, you might ask? Well, apparently a lot of folks, as I learned the hard way. My site got hacked 3 separate times until I got wise and switched to Option #1. I was even hacked by a

Malaysian anarchist group! And when a hacking occurs, it often means all of your hard work creating your website is GONE. I have several gray hairs that sprouted from this very experience. Don't go gray over your website. If you choose to create a Wordpress.com site, make sure you pay extra to protect it through some kind of anti-hacking backup service, like through the WinterWebMethod.com.

With this option, you will need to find a separate organization to host your site, like Pagely.com. Hosting by itself, and not bundled with other services, costs about $50-$100/year (Parr, 2015).

4. **The advanced techie route**: Build your website completely yourself with your amazing web design skills. If you are in this category, do not pass GO; do not collect $200; skip directly to the next section. You don't need my help with this! I bow down to your amazing tech prowess.

Whichever website route you choose, you will still be the one writing all of the content on it. Similar to building a new house, you can have architects and contractors design and build the entire thing, but they won't furnish it. The furnishing or writing is still up to you.

Search Engine Optimization (a.k.a. SEO)

SEO refers to getting your website to show up in search results when people go online looking for a therapist. There are many factors that affect how Google.com and other search engines will rank your site, including keywords, number of webpages, amount of unique content, etc., etc. Search engines basically scout out your website, and then decide how relevant and important it is. It's kind of a popularity contest to see which sites end up at the top of the search list, not too unlike electing a high school prom king. Just like that charming blond quarterback, you really want to win this contest. Think of when you're searching for something online. I'm willing to bet that you almost always click on links that show up only on the first page of your search.

> *"The best place to hide a dead body is page two of Google."*
> – Unknown

You want to set your website up for success to match what those search engines are looking for. There are entire books dedicated to understanding SEO, so I will not attempt to go into great detail about the subject here. It is important for you to know about it, and be aware of what you could do to help your website get seen. I suggest reading a book about the subject, such as *Search Engine Optimization for Dummies*.

Many agencies offer to provide SEO for you (for a fee, of course), often as an add-on to another service like web hosting. You may wish to take them up on that and see if you get positive results. A very useful tool in determining which keywords to sprinkle throughout your site to optimize it for search engines is the Keyword Planner on Google Adwords (Google.com/adwords). The best part is it's free! To get started, they have you create a new Adwords account. You will have to add a credit card, but it's never charged unless you actively run an Adwords campaign. Once you have an Adwords account, you can get keyword ideas and see how many people are searching for those words in your specific area.

Google Analytics is another great free tool that can help you determine how many people are clicking on your site and which pages are most popular. To get started with Analytics, you will add a secret hidden code to your website, and then it can work its magic. It's easier than it sounds. Check it out at Google.com/Analytics.

Online Directories

When you start looking into it, you'll find there are many online directories for therapists. A directory is a site where potential clients can search for nearby therapists, and filter results by using certain criteria that they are looking for.

The best one that I hear about time and again is PsychologyToday.com. I agree with the hype. PsychologyToday.com is a great, inexpensive way to boost your online profile, and has been the best investment I've made in my practice. It's $30 per month. And no, I don't work for them. I've had limited success with other directory sites, like GoodTherapy.org, but I think success may depend on your location. It makes sense to try other sites for brief periods to see if they work for you. Some may offer a free trial period for you to test it out.

There are other directories to think about, as well. Yelp.com and YellowPages.com are free places to register your business. If there is something you specialize in, you might be able to get registered in some directories for that specialty. For example, I got registered with several cancer support sites. Do an online search for therapists in your area to find out what sites and directories they are listed on; then add your name to them too.

Social Media

Having a Facebook and Twitter (and maybe Instagram, LinkedIn, etc.) page for your business should not be underestimated for their marketing power in this day and age. I must admit that I do not put as much energy into maintaining my social media presence as I would like to. I certainly recommend putting at least *some* effort into social media. Remember that every time you post something, your followers are reminded that you exist as a referral resource. To get pumped about social media, I recommend the book, *Crush It* by Gary Vaynerchuk.

I have heard from some folks who may be concerned about their personal social media profiles getting connected to their business profiles. Rest assured, there is a way to prevent your clients from seeing Facebook selfies of you chugging margaritas on the beach in your Speedo. You'll just want to make sure to adjust your privacy settings to only share what you want to share with only those you want to share it with. If you aren't sure how to do this, check out the help section on your preferred social media website. Better yet, ask someone under the age of 25. They will surely know.

Blogging

My husband happens to work in marketing, and I can't tell you the number of times he has encouraged me to blog. Do I follow his expert advice? Not nearly as much as I would like to. But I should, because having a blog on your website (and linked to your social media profiles) can greatly increase your search engine optimization (see above section on SEO). This means your website gets seen by more potential clients. And search engines reward sites that have new content by boosting them up the search results list. Don't worry that you aren't the utmost authority on a subject – you can still write about it. I bet you know a thing or two about something.

You should also consider doing guest blogs on other big websites such as GoodTherapy.org or PsychologyToday.com. If you have a subject you know a lot about, panda bear assisted therapy for example (pandas *do* seem like they'd be very therapeutic to cuddle with), contact one of these sites to see if they will let you post a guest blog on their site. There will be a link back to your website in the blog, which helps with SEO. And it gets your name out to a new, usually larger, set of readers. It's a win-win.

What kind of therapist are you?

More important than having a logo or marketing materials, is defining your niche. Time and again, you will hear people in this field talk about the importance of having a niche or specialty area to help you stand out from the crowd of other therapists. My initial fear, like so many others, was that I would alienate potential clients who did not fall into my narrow niche definition. However, many a therapist and business-savvy person has reassured me that this is not the case. Over the years, I have found that you will still get referrals from those with general depression, anxiety, adjustment disorder, and others who don't exactly fit your niche. I will reiterate what my wise forefathers and foremothers have said: "Don't be afraid of carving out your niche! It will help you, not harm you."

Choose your niche wisely from the start. I initially chose to market myself with a specialty in online counseling for cancer patients and their caregivers, as I had previously worked at a cancer center, and that is what I felt confident doing. With time, though, I've found that my passion lies more in working with trauma and codependency. And I don't do as much online counseling as I do face-to-face sessions. It has been an uphill battle to try to change the association of me in people's minds as "the online cancer therapist" to "the trauma and codependency therapist."

It may be difficult to know exactly what you want to focus on from the beginning, and that is ok. Don't let perfectionism paralyze you from choosing a niche. You *can* redefine yourself. It just takes a bit more work than creating an initial association in people's minds.

I will keep the discussion of choosing a specialty brief, as it could easily become a very lengthy tome. There are already some terrific resources out there for this aspect of growing your practice. One such resource for more in-depth advice about choosing a niche and developing your ideal client base is *Building Your Ideal Private Practice* by Lynn Grodzki. I would recommend it for every private practitioner's bookshelf – oh, and you should read it, not just put it on your shelf to collect dust.

The Black Hole of Waiting

I don't know about you, but I'm an extremely impatient person. That's part of the reason I got into private practice in the first place. I was sick of waiting around to get hired for the right job (it was really only a few weeks, but felt like an eternity). So, I took matters into my own hands, and made my own job. I just didn't think about one aspect of doing that—needing clients.

Getting clients isn't always completely within your control. Sure, there are countless things you can do to help with building your practice – many of which are mentioned above. But sometimes, you have to hurry up and wait for those things you did to take effect. Think of it like gardening; sometimes it can take a while for the seeds to bear fruit.

Even if you did everything right, there's a good chance you'll be stuck in limbo for a time, waiting for your very first client. The build-up leading up to this moment was exciting. You felt in control of your own destiny. You practiced visualizations of clients flooding your phone lines. Now you have officially stuck out your neck by announcing your new business to *every* person you know in the whole wide world. And yet – no one is calling. No one is filling out your fancy web form. Soon you jump at every phone call or email ding, hoping it will be that magical, elusive, first client. It's a high-stress time, to be sure.

It can be nearly impossible to maintain your optimism and passion, as you feel an awful dread gnawing in the pit of your stomach that no one is ever going to want to be your client. Maybe your idea was terrible, and you should have played it safe and waited for that so-so job offer to come along....

No one talks about this awkward period, but I'm nearly positive that everyone goes through it to some extent. The imposter syndrome is universal, especially when you're trying something new and out of your comfort zone. Hang in there! The calls *will* come. Practice self-care, distraction, positive thinking – use whatever therapeutic tools you've got in that toolbox of yours!

Chapter 6

I'm Relocating! Now What?

Moving your practice from one location to another can feel daunting. You worked so hard to build your initial practice; it seems unfair to have to start all over again! However, with our increasingly mobile society, relocation may be a reality for many of you. In fact, it became a reality for me. I moved my practice from Colorado to Oregon. I won't lie; it was no easy feat. But it is doable.

Here are some tidbits I learned along the way that may make your transition a little smoother:

- **Do your homework (in advance)** – I recommend looking into the local laws related to your specific type of licensure in the state or country you want to move to long before you actually move, if possible. As you likely have already encountered, licensing boards tend to move at their own snail-like pace. I'm sure they have their reasons for doing so, like lack of funding and staffing shortages, but boy can it be frustrating! Start the process of applying for licensure as soon as you can, as it will likely take several months, at least. You will need your new license before you can do much of anything in your new location.

- **Scope out the new digs** – You will want to do your research on your new location, just like you did for your previous area. Collecting data about demographics and other therapists is vital for you to do before you choose a new space. Revisit my previous chapter, "Office Logistics" to refresh your memory on how to effectively pick out a locale for your office.

- **Get an address ASAP** – Having a physical office address in your new area is one of the most important first steps to changing zip codes. You can't update any insurance or EAP contracts without it. You can't get mail forwarded without it. You can't see clients without it.

You may want to wait until you arrive in your new place before settling on a new office space. When I relocated, I was determined to get a jump on things so I could begin working (and earning money) as soon as I could. I mentioned I am not a patient person, right?

I was unable to visit the new place to physically see an office space, so I used online video conferencing to do a virtual tour of the space with the landlord. I also used the street view image feature in Google Maps to virtually walk down the street where my new office space was located. Thank goodness for technology! I will say, I did not sign a lease or pay a deposit until I physically saw the office. I would recommend holding out like this if you can.

- **Update insurance** – If you do not accept insurance, you can go ahead and skip this section. Otherwise, you will need to do the tedious work of updating your new contact information and licensure with insurance and EAP companies. Ack! Cue a violent storm of forms, faxing, and emails! Where to begin?

Start by updating your CAQH account, which some insurance companies use to stay up to date. You will have to sign a new contract with each insurance company, and your rates may change. This may be a good opportunity to try to negotiate a rate increase. Yes, you can (and should) negotiate with insurance companies. This is something I did not inherently know and had to be told. It can help you earn hundreds (maybe thousands) more over the long-term. Don't be afraid of asking for more. Lord knows they lowball the hell out of us.

Beware of two things:

1. This process of updating insurance contracts appears simple on the surface, but it is lengthy and often requires some back and forth with the company to get it all squared away.

2. You are not considered "in-network" for the new state until the contracts have been updated.

I also recommend researching ahead of time which insurance and EAP companies are popular in your new location. I was under the mistaken assumption that the same large insurance companies covering clients in my previous location would be the same ones in my new location. In actuality, there are many small, region-specific insurance companies out there.

How can you figure out which insurance or EAP companies are popular? Revisit my section on "Getting Started" with insurance companies in Chapter 4. Once you have determined which insurance companies are popular, you may wish to apply to join their networks.

- **Slow your roll** – Expect the whole process to take a long time, even if you are speedy about completing your part of the relocation procedures. Moving involves a lot of waiting on bureaucracy. If you expect it to take a long time, you might be pleasantly surprised when things come to fruition sooner than you expected. How nice to be pleasantly surprised, as opposed to frustrated when your practice isn't up and running a month after you arrive in your new location? Was that a therapeutic technique I just used there?

  Make sure you have a decent cushion in your savings account or are otherwise independently wealthy (lucky you!) to weather the wait for your practice to get back in action. Because every practice is unique, I can't recommend any certain length of time that you will need to rely on your savings. In a general sense, having a stash of about six-months' worth of salary in your savings is probably a good idea.

- **Have faith** – You did it before, and you can do it again! It can be incredibly scary to strike out into uncharted territory and set up shop again. Think of how much more knowledge and experience you have in doing it the second time, though. It could be a chance to reinvent your practice, now that you are older and wiser. Know that clients will show up, and it will happen faster than it did the first time because you know more about how to make it happen.

Chapter 7
How Do I Manage My Schedule?

How many clients should I have per week?

This is an eternally controversial question amongst folks in this field. I have run into people who swear that seeing any more than 10 clients per week is unethical. And I have heard folks say that if you're seeing less than 40 clients per week, you're a slacker who will never make money. Just kidding - therapists would never say something so mean. But they will certainly imply it.

You need to find your sweet spot of how many clients you feel good about seeing. Different people have different burnout levels. I tend to lean towards having fewer clients per week. If I am working full-time, I will generally schedule five client appointment slots per workday or 25 clients per week. I schedule them mostly back-to-back to optimize my time in the office. I find that my brain starts to go blank after my fifth client of the day. If I notice I'm searching for words in my head and they won't connect with my mouth, I know I've hit my max. Listen to your brain and your body when they cry, "Uncle!" and cut back your hours as needed.

Also, client stamina does build up over time somewhat. So, you may be able to see more clients after your practice is more established. No matter how many client slots you choose to have, you must figure in that you will likely have a few no-shows and late cancellations during your week.

Here is one scheduling trick I learned from a wise therapist and business coach to maximize your time: schedule two 45-minute sessions back to back, and then take a 15-minute break after that. Doing this, you would have a 90-minute block of time without breaks. The thought is that you could see two clients in 90-minutes, when it would usually take 2 hours. This is especially relevant for therapists taking insurance and EAP payments, as 45-minutes is all the time they are paying for.*

I have to admit, I have not utilized this strategy very often. I enjoy my snacking and bathroom breaks in between traditional 50-mintue sessions. And to pull this off, you need to be very disciplined about ending sessions on time, which I am not (a bad habit, I know!). But it may work well for you, so I encourage you to try it. Building a private practice is all about trial and error. What works well for one clinician may not work at all for someone else – just like counseling techniques. You get to personalize your practice like your very own Subway sandwich, only tastier.

*A Note About Billing

Here are the most often used Current Procedural Terminology (CPT) billing codes to consider when submitting a claim:

- 90791: Psychiatric Diagnostic evaluation
- 90834: Psychotherapy with patient and/or family member, 38-52 minutes
- 90837: Psychotherapy with patient and/or family member, 53+ minutes
- 90847: Family psychotherapy, conjoint with the patient present, no time listed

Medicaid, Medicare, and some insurance companies will pay for the longer 90837 code with no questions asked, although not all of them pay a higher amount compared to the 90834 code. Some companies require a prior authorization with a stated medical reason about why a longer session is needed. An example of a time when a longer session is needed is the use of specialized trauma treatment, eye movement desensitization and reprocessing (EMDR). And still other companies won't pay for the longer sessions no matter what.

What's a therapist to do? Ask! Always ask ahead of time when you contact the insurance company to verify a new client's eligibility. You can run several potential CPT codes by them to see what they will cover before you go to submit any claims.

There is confusion about when to use the 90847 family psychotherapy billing code. This is my understanding from gathering all of the information that I could about this topic:

- First off, to be able to bill insurance for anything, including family therapy, your identified patient must have a diagnosable disorder from the DSM. Z-Codes for life stressors do not count to insurance companies. I think there should be a Z-code for stress caused by insurance billing for therapists.

- Secondly, the 90847 code should be used when the focus of treatment overall is the family and family dynamics. The sessions should involve family participation from more than one family member.

- This is different from the individual psychotherapy codes (90834 & 90837), in which the focus of treatment is on the individual, and may, at times, involve bringing in a family member to a session.

Don't hesitate to utilize other appropriate codes for your work beyond those listed above. For many years, I didn't know I could bill for services like case management or even an add-on code for "interactive complexity" when a session involves a translator or other third party. Make sure you are aware of which codes you can bill for. Get paid accurately for the hard work that you do!

CPT Codes get updated each year in October by the American Medical Association (AMA). The AMA has a limited free CPT code search page on their website (https://www.ama-assn.org/). It may be more helpful, though, to search the web for CPT questions you have, as there are many websites specifically geared towards therapists.

A solid cancellation policy is worth its weight in gold
Late cancellations and no-shows can become the bane of any therapist's existence. When I first started as a therapist, I was shocked by how little regard people seemed to have for a scheduled appointment. Being the Type-A people-pleaser that I am, it had never even occurred to me to not show up for an appointment I had made. I learned very quickly that this adherence to the rules is not a universal mindset.

The truth is you will have a lot of late cancelations and no-shows. A lot. At first, it will probably offend you, frustrate you, anger you, even lower your self-esteem. Fight that urge! It is not about you. If you are coming from another therapist job in an agency or elsewhere, you will likely know this in advance, which is good.

What can you do about it? Establish a solid cancelation policy. Then, enforce it with consistency. Do I hear the B-word we love to use so much in counseling? I'm talking about boundaries, folks.

My policy is that clients must give 24-hours-notice to reschedule or cancel. Otherwise, there is a $40 cancelation fee. If they are ok with it, I get my clients' signature permitting me to securely store their credit card on file for copays and for cancelation fees if they come up. I am lenient on first-time cancelations and illness, and I often waive my fee for those cases.

It is a fine line between asserting your boundary and alienating a truly sick client who will not return for another session because they're frustrated by your policy. It's a tough balance to strike. I've heard of other therapists who are much more firm in their boundaries, and charge the full session fee for any cancelation. As I have said before, try a policy on for size, and see if it fits for you. Make sure you have some sort of policy that you communicate clearly both verbally and in writing.

I also mentioned previously that I use a medical records software program (Simple Practice) that sends out automatic session reminder emails to clients. I have it set to send both an email reminder 72 hours in advance, and phone reminder 48 hours in advance to clients. I can't tell you how much money I've saved by avoiding no-shows from this!

Final Thoughts

I hope that you find this road map to be helpful as you begin your private practice journey. I have confidence that you have smartly saved yourself much of the stress and time lost that I experienced trying to forage for this information piecemeal on my own.

Too often, we turn business into an "every man (or woman) for himself" affair. We think of our colleagues as our competition, rather than our allies. This way of thinking is an unfortunate mistake. Collective wisdom and collaboration is where business growth can flourish. So, as you forge ahead and learn more about this ever-changing career, I hope you will share your knowledge with those around you. Let your friends and colleagues know if you find a shortcut or strategy for streamlining your process.

On that note, I also want to remind you that being in business means always being in flux. The most important trait to have in this field is adaptability. If you stop trying to improve your practice in some way or another, you will become stagnant. This is a surefire way for a business to not only become boring for its owner, but also to eventually fail to keep up with changing times in the long-term.

You must remain agile and continue to educate yourself on shifting tides in the economy, technology, treatment techniques, etc. Participate in continuing education (you have to in order to maintain a license anyway). Talk to a young person about what new apps they use on their devices. Follow politics related to changes in healthcare, and get involved if you don't like what you see. Create a new form to better streamline your intake process. This is what keeps us inspired and engaged, rather than asleep at our desks in a puddle of drool.

I am inspired by the good work of helping people live better lives that you do each and every day. Go forth and heal those who need it most, my fellow comrades!

Appendix A

To Do List

I love lists! I hope this one helps you organize your thoughts about where to start with the, seemingly overwhelming, tasks of starting a practice. This list is written in the rough order in which I would recommend completing these tasks. Feel free to alter the order as you see fit.

- ❑ Decide on a name for your practice
- ❑ Apply for your business entity status (LLC, Sole Proprietor, etc.)
- ❑ Register as a new business in your county, if applicable
- ❑ Purchase a domain name
- ❑ Choose a website host and method of website development
- ❑ Create your website
- ❑ Locate an office space and sign a lease
- ❑ Create an email account
- ❑ Set up a phone number
- ❑ Get a P.O. Box, if applicable
- ❑ Order business cards
- ❑ Apply for insurance and/or EAP panels – Approval can take many months, so have patience.
- ❑ Open a business checking account
- ❑ Purchase office supplies
- ❑ Set up credit card billing
- ❑ Purchase office furniture/décor if needed
- ❑ Create standard forms – intake, disclosure, ROI
- ❑ Create social media profiles – Facebook, Twitter, Instagram, etc.
- ❑ Begin marketing – Psychology Today, networking, social media, etc.
- ❑ See your first client!!
- ❑ Purchase a scheduling/electronic medical records account (like Simple Practice) – You can hold off on this for awhile until you have a steady flow of clients. You can use password protected Word or Google documents and a standard online calendar or even an old school paper calendar at first.
- ❑ Subscribe to a video conferencing platform, if applicable

Appendix B
What to Buy

There are some items you will need to purchase for your practice, some which are optional. I have created this shopping list for you. Keep in mind, you don't have to purchase everything all at once. You can wait until you've built up a cushion in your business bank account for many of these items. You may also be able to go on a scavenger hunt for several items around your house. Or, if you share an office, that could nix the office décor section.

- ❏ Office Supplies
    - o Computer
    - o Printer/scanner/fax machine
    - o Paper shredder
    - o Business cards
    - o Business card holder - optional
    - o Address labels
    - o Ink cartridges
    - o Paper – Printer, lined, and notepads
    - o Envelopes
    - o Postage stamps
    - o Pens
    - o Paper clips
    - o Stapler and staples
    - o Clipboards (2-3)
    - o Tissues
- ❏ Laptop bag for travel to and from the office
- ❏ Sign for outside your office – optional. Vistaprint is a good place to shop for one.
- ❏ Office Décor
    - o Clock(s) – I have more than one so I that I can surreptitiously check the time without clients noticing.
    - o Desk
    - o Chairs
    - o Bookshelf

- Curtains and curtain rods, if needed
- Wall art
- Rug, if needed
- Lamps
- Lightbulbs
- White noise machines – 2, one for inside the office and one for outside
- A "Quiet Please" sign for your office door. You'd be amazed at how loud passersby can be! You could make your own sign on the computer or by getting supplies at a craft store.

Appendix C

Anticipated Business Expenses

This is based on expenses for my business located in Denver, Colorado. I am using it here to give you a very rough estimate of what your costs may be like in your practice. Obviously, expenses would vary significantly based on many factors, such as office location, state fees, preferences for spending on optional items, etc.

Item	Estimated Monthly Cost	Estimated Annual Cost
Office Space Rent (Full time)	$400 (Varies greatly by location)	$4,800
Practice Management Software	$27	$320
Marketing – PsychologyToday.com	$29.95	$659
Marketing – Website	$12.50	$150
Marketing – Other	Sky's the limit	Sky's the limit
Networking Events and Meet-ups	$10	$120
Accounting – Annual Tax Preparation	$42	$500
Accounting – "Keeping the books"	$20	$240
Accounting – Quickbooks desktop version	$6	$64
Credit Card/Bank Fees	$55	$660
Google Apps for Business	$5	$60
Secretary of State Business Registry	<$1	$10 (depends on state fees)
State Licensure Fees	$5.30	$64 (depends on state fees)
Liability Insurance	$30	$360
Office Supplies	$10	$120
Continuing Education	Sky's the limit	Sky's the limit

	Monthly	Annual
Totals:	$653.75+	$8,127+

Appendix D

Tax Deductible Items

Taxes are high for the self-employed. Therefore, you're going to want to make sure you deduct any legitimate business expense you can from your taxes. Here is a list of items that may be tax deductible. There may be items that are not on this list, but could still qualify as a deductible expense. Always verify your deductions with your accountant and keep your receipts to prove these deductions are legitimate in case the IRS comes calling.

- Office space rent
- Office supplies
- Office furniture and décor
- Phone bill – If you use your personal cell phone as your business phone as well, a portion of your cell phone bill can be written off. Estimate what percentage of your phone usage is business-related.
- Mileage – This is a tricky one, folks. Mileage to and from your office for regular work days is NOT deductible, unfortunately. However, mileage for other things, like going to the bank, library, consult groups, supervision, post office, networking meetups, and other business-related tasks is deductible. I recommend keeping track of your mileage in a little notebook in your car.
- Food and drinks from networking meetings at restaurants or coffee shops
- Professional development trainings
- Professional licensure fees
- State business registration fees
- Professional liability insurance
- Marketing costs
- Business cards
- Accounting fees
- Bank and credit card processing fees
- Books related to your practice
- Cleaning supplies
- Light bulbs

Appendix E
Intake Form Template

I usually email intake and disclosure forms to clients when they schedule their first appointment. I request that they either print them out and complete them ahead of time, or show up 15 minutes early to their initial session to complete it in the waiting area.

Many of the screening questions on the intake form are taken from the Screening, Brief Intervention, and Referral to Treatment (SBIRT) model. SBIRT is an evidence-based practice used to identify, reduce, and prevent substance use disorders (SAMHSA, 2017). A few of these standardized questions also aim to identify anxiety and depression issues. SBIRT was originally designed for a primary care setting, but can be very helpful in a therapy practice, as well.

The SBIRT model suggests that providers should follow up any positive screening question responses with further intervention. In addition to your excellent assessment interviewing skills, you may want to consider using additional validated screening tools to further flush out substance use and mental health issues. There are many helpful tools out there, but here are the four that I use most often as a follow up to the screening questions:

- The Alcohol Use Disorders Identification Test (AUDIT) for alcohol use - https://www.drugabuse.gov/sites/default/files/files/AUDIT.pdf
- The Drug Abuse Screening Test (DAST) for drug use - https://www.drugabuse.gov/sites/default/files/files/DAST-10.pdf
- The Patient Health Questionnaire (PHQ-9) for depression symptoms - http://www.agencymeddirectors.wa.gov/files/AssessmentTools/14-PHQ-9%20overview.pdf
- The Generalized Anxiety Disorder Scale (GAD-7) for anxiety symptoms - http://www.integration.samhsa.gov/clinical-practice/GAD708.19.08Cartwright.pdf

If you are interested in learning more about SBIRT, please visit http://www.integration.samhsa.gov/clinical-practice/sbirt.

Client Information

Date:_____

Legal Name:_____ Preferred Name:_____

Phone:_____ Messages OK (Y/N)? _____

Email:_____

Address:_____

DOB:_____/_____/_____

Occupation:_____

How did you find out about us?_____

. * . * . * . * . * . * . * . * . * . * . * . * . * .

Emergency Contact

_____ (Initials) I agree that *BUSINESS NAME* may contact this person in case of emergency.

Name:_____ Relationship:_____

Phone:_____

Address:_____

City:_____ State:_____ Zip:_____

. * . * . * . * . * . * . * . * . * . * . * . * . * .

Client Questions

All answers will be kept confidential, except in cases of threat of harm to self or others, known or suspected child or elder abuse, or court order.

• **Have you ever received a mental health diagnosis?** ☐ Yes ☐ No   If yes, what was it?
• **Have you <u>ever</u> taken medications for a mental health or emotional issue?** ☐ Yes ☐ No   If yes, which ones?
• **Have you ever been hospitalized for mental health or emotional reasons?** ☐ Yes ☐ No
• **Have you ever had an eating disorder or compulsive habit (gambling, shopping, etc.)** ☐ Yes ☐ No
• **Have you had any thoughts about harming yourself or others?**   ☐ Current/recent thoughts ☐ Past thoughts ☐ Never
• **Do you have any legal issues right now?** ☐ Yes ☐ No

Are you currently pregnant (for women)? ☐ Yes ☐ No

Alcohol: When answering the following questions, 1 drink will be considered: **12 oz. beer, 5 oz. wine; 1½ oz. liquor.**

1. How often do you have a drink containing alcohol?

2. How often do you have 4 (for women/men >65 yrs.)/5 (for men) or more drinks on one occasion?

   When was the last time you had 4(for women/men >65 yrs.)/5 (for men) or more drinks in one occasion?

3. How many drinks do you have per week?

Drugs:

1. How many times in the past year have you used marijuana? _____

2. In the past year, have you used or experimented with an illegal drug or a prescription drug for non- medical reasons?

   ☐ Yes ☐ No

Depression:

1. Over the past six months have you experienced a **2 week** period of time where you have felt down, depressed, or hopeless?

   ☐ Yes ☐ No

2. Over the past six months have you experienced a **2 week** period of time where you have felt little interest or pleasure in doing things?

   ☐ Yes ☐ No

Anxiety:
Over the past 2 weeks, how often have you been bothered by the following problems? (Circle one number)

1. Feeling nervous, anxious, or on edge?
   - **0** Not at all
   - **1** Several days
   - **2** More than half the days
   - **3** Nearly every day

2. Not being able to stop or control worry?
   - **0** Not at all
   - **1** Several days
   - **2** More than half the days
   - **3** Nearly every day

Appendix F

Disclosure Form Template

<u>Disclosure Statement & Policies</u>

My Education & Credentials

LIST YOUR DEGREE AND OTHER CREDENTIALS HERE.

Philosophy & Approach: *DESCRIBE THEORIES AND TECHNIQUES YOU USE.*

ADJUST TO YOUR STATE'S REQUIRED STATEMENT: As a licensee of the Oregon Board of Licensed Professional Counselors and Therapists, I abide by its Code of Ethics. To maintain my license, I am required to participate in continuing education, taking classes dealing with subjects relevant to this profession.

As a client of an Oregon licensee, you have the following rights:

- To expect that a licensee has met the qualifications of training and experience required by state law;
- To examine public records maintained by the Board and to have the Board confirm credentials of a licensee;
- To obtain a copy of the Code of Ethics (Oregon Administrative Rules 833-100);
- To report complaints to the Board;
- To be informed of the cost of professional services before receiving the services;
- To be assured of privacy and confidentiality while receiving services as defined by rule or law, with the following exceptions: 1) Reporting suspected child abuse; 2) Reporting imminent danger to you or others; 3) Reporting information required in court proceedings or by your insurance company, or other relevant agencies; 4) Providing information concerning licensee case consultation or supervision; and 5) Defending claims brought by you against me;
- To be free from discrimination because of age, color, culture, disability, ethnicity, national origin, gender, race, religion, sexual orientation, marital status, or socioeconomic status.

You may contact the Board of Licensed Professional Counselors and Therapists at **3218 Pringle Rd SE, #250, Salem, OR 97302-6312, Telephone: (503) 378-5499, Email:** lpct.board@state.or.us, Website: www.oregon.gov/OBLPCT. For additional information about this licensee, consult the Board's website.

Emails: Emails can be used for asking simple questions, asking about rescheduling a time, a quick update, etc. Email may also be used for appointment reminders and self-help information. A HIPAA-compliant program called Simple Practice may be used to schedule sessions and communicate reminders. Please indicate whether or not you would like to participate in this kind of communication:

☐ **Yes**   ☐ **No**

I do offer email counseling, as well. Emails involving requests for advice, guidance, to be listened to, or any other therapeutic reasons are considered email counseling. There will be an invoiced charge for this type of email.

Record Keeping: I will keep brief records of our sessions. Under the provisions of the Health Care Information Act of 1992, you have the right to a copy of your file at any time. You have the right to request that I correct any errors in your file. You have the right to request that I make a copy of your file available to any other health care provider at your written request.

Limitations of Services: I do not offer 24-hour care. If you need after-hours care, I will assist you in finding the proper resources. If you have an emergency, you need to contact your local emergency room or call 911.

Ending Counseling: You normally will be the one who decides counseling will end, with a few exceptions:

• If I am not, in my judgment, able to help you because of the kind of problem you have or because my training and skills are not appropriate, I will inform you of this fact and refer you to another therapist who may meet your needs.

- If you are violent or threatening toward myself, my office, or my family, I reserve the right to terminate you unilaterally and immediately from treatment.
- If you miss 2 or more sessions without at least 24 hours notice, I reserve the right to terminate therapy with you.
- If I end counseling with you, I will offer you referrals to other sources of care, but cannot guarantee that they will accept you for therapy.

Cancelations: Cancelations/rescheduling must be arranged at least **24 hours before the session by phone**. If a session is missed or canceled/rescheduled within 24 hours of the session, you will be charged a **$40 cancelation fee**. An EAP or insurance may *not* pay for the late cancel or missed appointment. In case of inclement weather, a challenge with transportation, or any reason you are unable to reach my office for an in-person session, you can opt to attend the session via phone. Otherwise, the session will be cancelled.

Fees: My fee is $100 for a 55-minute session. This fee may be reduced by utilizing insurance coverage or an EAP. I have a sliding scale of $90 for a 45-minute session for clients experiencing financial hardship.

Payments: Payments are due at the time of service for in-person sessions. Payment for video or phone sessions must be received prior to the session via credit, cash, or check. I reserve the right to release your information to a collections agency to collect unpaid fees, if necessary. **Outstanding fees denied or not otherwise covered by an insurance company or EAP will be the responsibility of the client.**

> _____ **(Initials)** I agree to allow *BUSINESS NAME* to store my debit or credit card information online in a secure and HIPAA-compliant database to more conveniently bill for session fees, copays, deductibles, and cancelation fees. You will be notified in person and/or via email when a charge is made to your card on file.

Session Length: Counseling sessions range in length from 45 to 55 minutes, depending on type of session, cost, and coverage.

Children: Children under 12 must be supervised outside of the session room by an adult during sessions.

Cell Phones: Please refrain from using cell phones during sessions. Please note that audio or video recording of sessions is not permitted.

By signing below, I hereby acknowledge that I have received and have been given an opportunity to read a copy of *BUSINESS NAME's* Notice of Privacy Practices, attached. I understand that if I have any questions regarding the Notice or my privacy rights, I can contact *YOUR NAME* at *000-000-0000*.

I have read the preceding information, it has also been provided verbally, and I understand my rights as a client and agree to comply with the policies.

Client Signature:_____ **Date:**_____

Client Name (printed):_____

Counselor Signature:_____ **Date:**_____

Counselor Name (printed): _____

THIS NOTICE DESCRIBES HOW MEDICAL INFORMATION ABOUT YOU MAY BE USED AND DISCLOSED AND HOW YOU CAN GET ACCESS TO THIS INFORMATION.

PLEASE REVIEW THIS NOTICE CAREFULLY.

Your health record contains personal information about you and your health. This information about you that may identify you and that relates to your past, present or future physical or mental health or condition and related health care services is referred to as Protected Health Information ("PHI"). This Notice of Privacy Practices describes how we may use and disclose your PHI in accordance with applicable law, including the Health Insurance Portability and Accountability Act ("HIPAA"), regulations promulgated under HIPAA including the HIPAA Privacy and Security Rules. It also describes your rights regarding how you may gain access to and control your PHI.

We are required by law to maintain the privacy of PHI and to provide you with notice of our legal duties and privacy practices with respect to PHI. We are required to abide by the terms of this Notice of Privacy Practices. We reserve the right to change the terms of our Notice of Privacy Practices at any time. Any new Notice of Privacy Practices will be effective for all PHI that we maintain at that time. We will provide you with a copy of the revised Notice of Privacy Practices by posting a copy on our website, sending a copy to you in the mail upon request or providing one to you at your next appointment.

HOW WE MAY USE AND DISCLOSE HEALTH INFORMATION ABOUT YOU

For Treatment. Your PHI may be used and disclosed by those who are involved in your care for the purpose of providing, coordinating, or managing your health care treatment and related services. This includes consultation with clinical supervisors or other treatment team members. We may disclose PHI to any other consultant only with your authorization.

For Payment. We may use and disclose PHI so that we can receive payment for the treatment services provided to you. This will only be done with your authorization. Examples of payment-related activities are: making a determination of eligibility or coverage for insurance benefits, processing claims with your insurance company, reviewing services provided to you to determine medical necessity, or undertaking utilization review activities. If it becomes necessary to use collection processes due to lack of payment for services, we will only disclose the minimum amount of PHI necessary for purposes of collection.

For Health Care Operations. We may use or disclose, as needed, your PHI in order to support our business activities including, but not limited to, quality assessment activities, employee review activities, licensing, and conducting or arranging for other business activities. For example, we may share your PHI with third parties that perform various business activities (e.g., billing or typing services) provided we have a written contract with the business that requires it to safeguard the privacy of your PHI. For training or teaching purposes PHI will be disclosed only with your authorization.

Required by Law. Under the law, we must disclose your PHI to you upon your request. In addition, we must make disclosures to the Secretary of the Department of Health and Human Services for the purpose of investigating or determining our compliance with the requirements of the Privacy Rule.

Without Authorization. Following is a list of the categories of uses and disclosures permitted by HIPAA without an authorization. Applicable law and ethical standards permit us to disclose information about you without your authorization only in a limited number of situations.

As a counselor licensed in this state, it is our practice to adhere to more stringent privacy requirements for disclosures without an authorization. The following language addresses these categories.

Child or Elder Abuse or Neglect. We may disclose your PHI to a state or local agency that is authorized by law to receive reports of child abuse or neglect.

Judicial and Administrative Proceedings. We may disclose your PHI pursuant to a subpoena (with your written consent), court order, administrative order or similar process.

Deceased Patients. We may disclose PHI regarding deceased patients as mandated by state law, or to a family member or friend that was involved in your care or payment for care prior to death, based on your prior consent. A release of information regarding deceased patients may be limited to an executor or administrator of a deceased person's estate or the person identified as next-of-kin. PHI of persons that have been deceased for more than fifty (50) years is not protected under HIPAA.

Medical Emergencies. We may use or disclose your PHI in a medical emergency situation to medical personnel only in order to prevent serious harm. Our staff will try to provide you a copy of this notice as soon as reasonably practicable after the resolution of the emergency.

Family Involvement in Care. We may disclose information to close family members or friends directly involved in your treatment based on your consent or as necessary to prevent serious harm.

Health Oversight. If required, we may disclose PHI to a health oversight agency for activities authorized by law, such as audits, investigations, and inspections. Oversight agencies seeking this information include government agencies and organizations that provide financial assistance to the program (such as third-party payors based on your prior consent) and peer review organizations performing utilization and quality control.

Law Enforcement. We may disclose PHI to a law enforcement official as required by law, in compliance with a subpoena (with your written consent), court order, administrative order or similar document, for the purpose of identifying a suspect, material witness or missing person, in connection with the victim of a crime, in connection with a deceased person, in connection with the reporting of a crime in an emergency, or in connection with a crime on the premises.

Specialized Government Functions. We may review requests from U.S. military command authorities if you have served as a member of the armed forces, authorized officials for national security and intelligence reasons and to the Department of State for medical suitability determinations, and disclose your PHI based on your written consent, mandatory disclosure laws and the need to prevent serious harm.

Public Health. If required, we may use or disclose your PHI for mandatory public health activities to a public health authority authorized by law to collect or receive such information for the purpose of preventing or controlling disease, injury, or disability, or if directed by a public health authority, to a government agency that is collaborating with that public health authority.

Public Safety. We may disclose your PHI if necessary to prevent or lessen a serious and imminent threat to the health or safety of a person or the public. If information is disclosed to prevent or lessen a serious threat it will be disclosed to a person or persons reasonably able to prevent or lessen the threat, including the target of the threat.

Research. PHI may only be disclosed after a special approval process or with your authorization.

Verbal Permission. We may also use or disclose your information to family members that are directly involved in your treatment with your verbal permission.

With Authorization. Uses and disclosures not specifically permitted by applicable law will be made only with your written authorization, which may be revoked at any time, except to the extent that we have already made a use or disclosure based upon your authorization. The following uses and disclosures will be made only with your written authorization: (i) most uses and disclosures of psychotherapy notes which are separated from the rest of your medical record; (ii) most uses and disclosures of PHI for marketing purposes, including subsidized treatment communications; (iii) disclosures that constitute a sale of PHI; and (iv) other uses and disclosures not described in this Notice of Privacy Practices.

YOUR RIGHTS REGARDING YOUR PHI

You have the following rights regarding PHI we maintain about you. To exercise any of these rights, please submit your request in writing to our Privacy Officer at *BUSINESS NAME AND ADDRESS*:

- **Right of Access to Inspect and Copy.** You have the right, which may be restricted only in exceptional circumstances, to inspect and copy PHI that is maintained in a "designated record set". A designated record set contains mental health/medical and billing records and any other records that are used to make decisions about your care. Your right to inspect and copy PHI will be restricted only in those situations where there is compelling evidence that access would cause serious harm to you or if the information is contained in separately maintained psychotherapy notes. We may charge a reasonable, cost-based fee for copies. If your records are maintained electronically, you may also request an electronic copy of your PHI. You may also request that a copy of your PHI be provided to another person.

- **Right to Amend.** If you feel that the PHI we have about you is incorrect or incomplete, you may ask us to amend the information although we are not required to agree to the amendment. If we deny your request for amendment, you have the right to file a statement of disagreement with us. We may prepare a rebuttal to your statement and will provide you with a copy. Please contact the Privacy Officer if you have any questions.

- **Right to an Accounting of Disclosures.** You have the right to request an accounting of certain of the disclosures that we make of your PHI. We may charge you a reasonable fee if you request more than one accounting in any 12-month period.

- **Right to Request Restrictions.** You have the right to request a restriction or limitation on the use or disclosure of your PHI for treatment, payment, or health care operations. We are not required to agree to your request unless the request is to restrict disclosure of PHI to a health plan for purposes of carrying out payment or health care operations, and the PHI pertains to a health care item or service that you paid for out of pocket. In that case, we are required to honor your request for a restriction.

- **Right to Request Confidential Communication.** You have the right to request that we communicate with you about health matters in a certain way or at a certain location. We will accommodate reasonable requests. We may require information regarding how payment will be handled or specification of an alternative address or other method of contact as a condition for accommodating your request. We will not ask you for an explanation of why you are making the request.

- **Breach Notification.** If there is a breach of unsecured PHI concerning you, we may be required to notify you of this breach, including what happened and what you can do to protect yourself.

- **Right to a Copy of this Notice.** You have the right to a copy of this notice.

COMPLAINTS

If you believe we have violated your privacy rights, you have the right to file a complaint in writing with our Privacy Officer at *BUSINESS NAME AND ADDRESS* or with the Secretary of Health and Human Services at 200 Independence Avenue, S.W. Washington, D.C. 20201 or by calling (202) 619-0257. **We will not retaliate against you for filing a complaint.**

The effective date of this Notice is May 2014.

Release of Information

I,_____ whose date of birth is _____ , authorize

BUSINESS NAME to disclose to and/or obtain from

_____   Phone: _____

[Insert Name of Person or Organization]
the following information:
Description of Information to be Disclosed
(Client should initial each item to be disclosed)

_____	Assessment	_____	Educational Information
_____	Diagnosis	_____	Discharge/Transfer Summary
_____	Psychosocial Evaluation	_____	Continuing Care Plan
_____	Psychological Evaluation	_____	Progress in Treatment
_____	Psychiatric Evaluation	_____	Demographic Information
_____	Treatment Plan or Summary	_____	Emergency Contact
_____	Current Treatment Update	_____	Psychotherapy Notes*

_____ Medication Management Information

_____ Presence/Participation in Treatment

_____ Nursing/Medical Information

(*Cannot be combined with any other disclosure)

_____Other_____

_____Other_____

Purpose: The purpose of this disclosure of information is to improve assessment and treatment planning, share information relevant to treatment and when appropriate, coordinate treatment services.

Revocation: I understand that I have a right to revoke this authorization, in writing, at any time by sending written notification to *BUSINESS NAME AND ADDRESS*. I further understand that a revocation of the authorization is not effective to the extent that action has been taken in reliance on the authorization.

Expiration: Unless sooner revoked, this authorization expires on the following date: _____ or as otherwise indicated:_____.

Conditions: I further understand that *BUSINESS NAME* will not condition my treatment on whether I give authorization for the requested disclosure. However, it has been explained to me that failure to sign this authorization may have the following consequences: _____.

Form of Disclosure: Unless you have specifically requested in writing that the disclosure be made in a certain format, we reserve the right to disclose information as permitted by this authorization in any manner that we deem to be appropriate and consistent with applicable law, including, but not limited to, verbally, in paper format or electronically.

<u>Redisclosure</u>: I understand that there is the potential that the protected health information that is disclosed pursuant to this authorization may be redisclosed by the recipient and the protected health information will no longer be protected by the HIPAA privacy regulations, unless a State law applies that is more strict than HIPAA and provides additional privacy protections.

I will be given a copy of this authorization for my records.

_____

Signature of Client   Date

_____

Signature of Parent, Guardian or Personal Representative   Date

If you are signing as a personal representative of an individual, please describe your authority to act for this individual (power of attorney, healthcare surrogate, etc.).

_____

Signature of Staff Witness   Date

Treatment Plan Template

Client Name: _____

Date:_____

Area of Focus: _____

What I want:

_____

_____

_____

_____

Objective:

_____

_____

_____

_____

Methods:

_____

_____

_____

_____

Client Signature:_____ Date: _____

Therapist Signature:_____ Date: _____

Appendix I
Fax Cover Sheet Template

Your Logo
Here

FAX

Date:_____

To:_____

Company:_____

Fax Number:_____

Phone Number:_____

Memo:

_____
_____
_____
_____
_____
_____
_____

BUSINESS NAME, ADDRESS, PHONE NUMBER

References

BizFilings.com. (2016). *S corporation advantages and disadvantages.*
http://www.bizfilings.com/learn/s-corporation-advantages-and-disadvantages.aspx.

Costhelper.com. (N.D.) *How much does setting up an LLC cost?*
http://smallbusiness.costhelper.com/llc.html.

Frankle, N. (2014). *Disability insurance coverage for the self-employed: How to get the right coverage.* Wealth Pilgrim. http://wealthpilgrim.com/disability-insurance-for-self-employed-guide/.

Huggins, R. (2016). *Therapy Business Line on the Cheap?: HIPAA and VoIP Services.*
https://personcenteredtech.com/2016/05/31/therapy-business-line-cheap-hipaa-voip-services/.

Internal Revenue Service. 17 Dec 2015. *Retirement savings for self-employed people.*
https://www.irs.gov/Retirement-Plans/Retirement-Plans-for-Self-Employed-People.

Parr, R. (2015). *How much does a website cost in 2015?* Executionists Blog.
http://www.executionists.com/blog/much-w.

SAMHSA. (2017). *SBIRT: Screening, Brief Intervention, and Referral to Treatment.*
http://www.integration.samhsa.gov/clinical-practice/sbirt.

SBA.gov. (2015). *Choose & register your business.* https://www.sba.gov/content/how-name-business

51595142R00054

Made in the USA
Middletown, DE
03 July 2019